ROBERT'S RULES OF ORDER,

AND

WHY IT MATTERS

FOR

COLLEGES AND

UNIVERSITIES TODAY

EDITED AND INTRODUCED BY

CHRISTOPHER P. LOSS

PRINCETON UNIVERSITY PRESS

PRINCETON & OXFORD

Based on the original version of POCKET MANUAL OF RULES OF
ORDER FOR DELIBERATIVE ASSEMBLIES by Henry Martyn Robert,
February 1876 (http://www.gutenberg.org/cache/epub/9097/pg9097.txt)

Published by Princeton University Press
41 William Street, Princeton, New Jersey 08540
6 Oxford Street, Woodstock, Oxfordshire OX20 1TR

press.princeton.edu

Library of Congress Cataloging-in-Publication Data

Names: Loss, Christopher P., editor. | Robert, Henry M. (Henry Martyn),
1837–1923. Pocket manual of rules of order for deliberative assemblies . . . |
Robert, Henry M. (Henry Martyn), 1837–1923. Robert's rules of order.
Title: Robert's Rules of Order, and why it matters for colleges and
universities today / edited and introduced by Christopher P. Loss.
Other titles: Rules of order
Description: Princeton : Princeton University Press, [2021] | "Based on the
original version of POCKET MANUAL OF RULES OF ORDER FOR
DELIBERATIVE ASSEMBLIES by Henry Martyn Robert, February
1876"—T.p. verso.
Identifiers: LCCN 2021017040 (print) | LCCN 2021017041 (ebook) |
ISBN 9780691222844 (Hardcover : acid-free paper) |
ISBN 9780691222851 (eBook)
Subjects: LCSH: Parliamentary practice—United States. | Democracy and
education—United States. | BISAC: EDUCATION / Reference |
BUSINESS & ECONOMICS / Business Communication / Meetings &
Presentations
Classification: LCC JF515 .R695 2021 (print) | LCC JF515 (ebook) |
DDC 060.4/2—dc23
LC record available at https://lccn.loc.gov/2021017040
LC ebook record available at https://lccn.loc.gov/2021017041

British Library Cataloging-in-Publication Data is available

Editorial: Peter Dougherty, Alena Chekanov
Production Editorial: Terri O'Prey
Text Design: Karl Spurzem
Jacket/Cover Design: Layla Mac Rory
Production: Erin Suydam
Publicity: Alyssa Sanford, Carmen Jimenez

This book has been composed in Arno Pro with Kepler Std

Printed on acid-free paper. ∞

Printed in the United States of America

10 9 8 7 6 5 4 3 2 1

CONTENTS

Introduction: The Organization Man   vii

Editor's Note   xxxiii

Robert's Rules of Order: Pocket Manual of Rules of
    Order for Deliberative Assemblies   1

Acknowledgments   117

INTRODUCTION:
THE ORGANIZATION MAN

The year 1876 was an epochal one in American politics and letters. Enterprising Philadelphians pulled off the Centennial International Exposition to widespread acclaim. Despite continued economic aftershocks from the Panic of 1873, triggered when twenty-five railroads defaulted on their debts, nearly 10 million visitors poured into the city that summer to celebrate the signing of the Declaration of Independence and the experiment in democratic governance it unleashed.[1]

That 1876 was also an election year added excitement to the Exposition and to the hope that the next president of the United States might lift the nation's politics out of the doldrums after a decade of scandal and corruption. The good feelings didn't last, however, when contested party conventions led to compromise candidates and another electoral crisis in November. Even though Democratic Rep. Samuel J. Tilden, of New York, had won the popular vote over Republican Governor Rutherford B. Hayes, of Ohio, Tilden lost the presidency after Congressional Democrats ceded twenty disputed electoral-college votes and a Tilden victory in exchange for the withdrawal of federal troops from the South, effectively ending Reconstruction and with it the possibility of full African American citizenship. The irony was thick. More ballots had been cast than in any previous election, yet the outcome—a

---

1. Richard White, *The Republic for Which It Stands: The United States during Reconstruction and the Gilded Age, 1865–1896* (New York: Oxford University Press, 2017), 266–67, 288–89.

discredited, many believed illegitimate chief executive in Hayes, intensified sectionalism, segregation, and racial violence—could not have been less democratic.[2]

The realization that democracy might not be attainable by relying on traditional political institutions marked the first of many challenges to confront the American people and their government during the Gilded Age, when a minimal state of "courts and parties" grew into a bureaucratic state of public, private, and voluntary associations.[3] The heyday of *laissez-faire* individualism, the late nineteenth century was also a time of economic booms and busts, class strife and stratification, demographic change and xenophobia, and of fierce struggles for women's and African Americans' rights. It was, in other words, a tumultuous time much like our own, when many Americans doubted whether social, political, and economic justice were even possible under free-market capitalism. Having grown tired of "politics as usual" and the vagaries of the so-called natural market, many Americans, then, as now, were searching for new ways to engage civil society and mobilize voluntary action in order to revive the nation's waning democratic creed.[4]

Then, as now, many wondered if the nation's colleges and universities could arouse the feelings of national belonging that so

2. White, *Republic for Which It Stands*, 207, 333. Other elections in which the winner of the popular vote lost the presidency include 1824, 1888, 2000, and 2016.

3. Stephen Skowronek, *Building A New American State: The Expansion of National Administrative Capacities, 1877–1920* (New York: Cambridge University Press, 1982); Brian Balogh, *The Associational State: American Governance in the Twentieth Century* (Philadelphia: University of Pennsylvania Press, 2015); Elisabeth Clemens, *Civic Gifts: Voluntarism and the Making of the American Nation-State* (Chicago: University of Chicago Press, 2020).

4. This comparison has been made many times. See, for example, Larry M. Bartels, *Unequal Democracy: The Political Economy of the New Gilded Age* (Princeton, NJ: Princeton University Press, 2010); Kay Lehman Schlozman and Henry E. Brady, *Unequal and Unrepresented: Political Inequality and the People's Voice in the New Gilded Age* (Princeton, NJ: Princeton University Press, 2018); and countless magazine and newspaper articles.

many Americans craved. In a polity ambivalent about big government interventions, and with antigovernment sentiment on the rise, the country's decentralized higher education network surfaced as one possible way to bridge the gap "between citizens and the state" and restore equanimity and dignity to America's enfeebled civic culture.[5]

One major question remained: Was the educational system up to the task?

Then, as now, the answer was, at best, a shaky Maybe.

Back then, the country's higher education system, in flux since before the Civil War, remained dominated by the old-time denominational college. But the college's blend of hoary religious proselytizing and rote classical training seemed out of step in a fast-changing society buffeted from every direction by the forces of modernity. In the opinion of a small group of self-anointed academic reformers—led by Andrew Dickson White, of Cornell; Charles W. Eliot, of Harvard; and Daniel Coit Gilman, of Johns Hopkins—the old-time college was no better prepared to deal with the social and political crises of modern life than it had been to deal with the crisis of disunion and war. What the country needed was a "real university," implored Eliot, in *The Atlantic Monthly*, in 1869, where "every subject should be taught . . . on a higher plane than elsewhere." The German university and its commitment to pure research was the aspiration, but not one achieved in America, where university-building, like state-building, was a patchwork affair. Using homegrown and imported material, and funding from government land grants and Gilded Age tycoons, academic reformers' plan for the American university gradually took shape. It would be a college but on a grander scale, with a diverse mission that united undergraduate, professional, and

---

5. Christopher P. Loss, *Between Citizens and the State: The Politics of American Higher Education in the 20th Century* (Princeton, NJ: Princeton University Press, 2012).

doctoral training; nurtured disciplined inquiry; and generated expert knowledge to construct the nation anew.[6]

Easily the most revolutionary new university, and the one that, for a time, came closest to the German model, was Johns Hopkins University, opened in Baltimore, Maryland, in 1876, the same year that American democracy began to sputter and fume.[7] The date was a happy coincidence—local financier Johns Hopkins had died three years earlier, leaving half his $7 million estate for the creation of a namesake institution—subsequently seized upon by the school's president-in-waiting, Daniel Coit Gilman. Gilman, aged forty-four, had been in search of a real university for most of his adult life. After not finding what he was looking for at Yale (too hidebound) or the University of California (too political), Gilman landed in Baltimore. He was the world's leading expert on higher education before such a thing even existed. He had studied and traveled in Europe and spent time conducting research on research universities in the hope that he would someday get a chance to build one of his own. In careful and occasionally bold flourishes his inaugural address laid out the university's research, teaching, and service missions, before ending with an evocation of a possible expert-driven democratic renaissance: "This year is auspicious, inviting us to sink political animosities in sentiments of fraternal good will, and of patriotic regard for a re-united republic."[8]

---

6. Laurence R. Veysey, *The Emergence of the American University* (Chicago: University of Chicago Press, 1965); Roger L. Geiger, *The History of American Higher Education: Learning and Culture from the Founding to World War II* (Princeton, NJ: Princeton University Press, 2015), 316–26, quote on 319.

7. On the founding of Johns Hopkins, see Hugh Hawkins, *Pioneer: A History of the Johns Hopkins University, 1874–1889* (Ithaca, NY: Cornell University Press, 1960). For a reassessment, see Emily J. Levine, "Baltimore Teaches, Göttingen Learns: Cooperation, Competition, and the Research University," *American Historical Review* 121, no. 3 (June 2016): 780–823.

8. Gilman's inaugural address available at https://www.jhu.edu/about/history/gilman-address/.

A thousand miles away, in Milwaukee, Wisconsin, on the shores of Lake Michigan, Major Henry Martyn Robert, of the US Army Corps of Engineers, aged thirty-eight, was also pondering the dilemma of democratic nation-making and what he could do to fix it. Although he had a day job that kept him busy, he had just finished a small book on the side that he thought might help—not that anyone was holding their breath waiting to receive a free copy of *Robert's Rules of Order: Pocket Manual of Rules of Order for Deliberative Assemblies*.[9] He had never written a book before. He had no real audience of which to speak. And while he had an audience in mind, it wasn't clear that they'd be interested in what he had to say. All he knew was that democracy was in trouble and he felt duty-bound to try and save it. Remarkably, his rescue plan, if you could call it that, though far less grandiose than Gilman's, affected democratic norms on a day-to-day basis far more, and without setting out to do so, ultimately helped turn the American research university into a powerful engine of democracy for the nation and world.[10]

---

9. Henry M. Robert, *Robert's Rules of Order: Pocket Manual of Rules of Order for Deliberative Assemblies* (hereafter *RRO*) (Chicago: S. C. Griggs & Company, 1876). This edition was published in February 1876 and is the version included in this volume. Robert received his books on February 19, 1876; Gilman's inaugural speech was on February 22, 1876.

10. For Robert's biography I have relied on Ralph C. Smedley, *The Great Peacemaker* (Los Angeles: Borden Publishing Company, 1955); Ralph C. Smedley, *The Man Behind the Rules: An Account of the Life and Work of Henry Martyn Robert, author of Robert's Rules of Order* (Santa Ana, CA: Toastmasters International, 1937); Thais M. Plaisted, "General Henry M. Robert: Parliamentarian," *Social Studies* 48, no. 5 (May 1957): 158–62; E. J. Mehren, "Henry Martyn Robert: Soldier, Parliamentarian, Author and Engineer," *Engineering News-Record* 84, no. 17 (April 22, 1920): 798–802; the preface and introduction to Henry M. Robert, *Robert's Rules of Order, Newly Revised; a New and Enl. Ed. by Sarah Corbin Robert et al.,* (hereafter *RRONR*) (New York: Scott, Foresman and Company, 1970), xxi–xlii; and Don H. Doyle, "Rules of Order: Henry Martyn Robert and the Popularization of American Parliamentary Law," *American Quarterly* 32, no. 1 (Spring 1980): 3–18. On the connection between the university and democracy, see Loss, *Between Citizens and the State;* and Andrew Jewett, *Science, Democracy, and the American University: From the Civil War to the Cold War* (New York: Cambridge University Press, 2012).

* * *

The kernel of the idea for the book had been kicking around in Henry's head since the Civil War had torn the nation, and his family, in half. Henry was from South Carolina but had been raised all over the place, and he joined the Union Army even though it meant turning his slide rule against his relatives.[11] Henry was a civil engineer, one of the army's finest. He specialized in designing roads, bridges, causeways, canals, locks, jetties, and lighthouses, and, during the war, strategic fortifications around Washington, DC, and Philadelphia. These "internal improvements" helped save the Union and tie it back together later, linking one region to another and laying the groundwork for Western Conquest and the opening of new settlements and markets from sea-to-sea and beyond.[12]

Henry had been in constant motion since graduating near the top of his West Point class of 1857, moving wherever the Army Corps told him to be even when it meant leaving behind his wife, Helen, and their young children.[13] From his first assignment as a second lieutenant opening roads and bridges in the Pacific Northwest to his retirement as brigadier general and head of the Army Corps in 1901, Henry saw and did it all. His work took him deep into the country's interior, from the St. Lawrence Seaway to the

---

11. Henry had ten uncles who fought in the Confederate Army, including his mother's oldest brother, Brigadier General Alexander R. Lawton; see R. Frank Saunders Jr. and George A. Rogers, "Joseph Thomas Robert and the Wages of Conscience," *Georgia Historical Quarterly* 88, no. 1 (Spring 2004): 10–11.

12. Todd Shallat, *Structures in the Stream: Water, Science, and the Rise of the U.S. Army Corps of Engineers* (Austin: University of Texas Press, 1994); Theodore J. Crackel, *West Point: A Bicentennial History* (Lawrence: University Press of Kansas, 2002); Brian Balogh, *A Government Out of Sight: The Mystery of National Authority in Nineteenth-Century America* (New York: Cambridge University Press, 2009), 112–50.

13. See obituary for Mrs. Helen M. Robert, *The Dayton Herald*, October 16, 1895, available at https://www.newspapers.com/clip/27461047/1895-10-16-mrs-helen-m -robert-the/.

Gulf of Mexico, up and down both coasts and to all points between, and, on several occasions, for short teaching assignments at West Point.[14] He served on a host of national engineering boards, and his talents remained in heavy demand long after he retired from the army, right up until his death, in 1923, at the age of eighty-six. The Galveston Seawall was his greatest engineering feat: three miles of reinforced concrete (later expanded to ten miles) built after the 1900 hurricane destroyed the island and eight thousand lives. It has protected Galveston and the mainland ever since.[15]

Throughout his career, Henry dedicated most of his waking hours to studying hydrodynamics and whatever spare time he could muster thinking about the less predictable human dynamics of deliberative assemblies. Henry retraced his obsession with deliberative assemblies to a traumatic encounter in New Bedford, Massachusetts, in 1863, where he had been sent the year before to work on harbor construction and recuperate from a chronic bout of malaria contracted on his first Corps tour. Henry was a devout Baptist who religiously attended church services and participated in the YMCA whenever he could. On this occasion, he was asked to preside over a meeting at the First Baptist Church. The meeting quickly veered out of control. He had no idea how to chair it. "My embarrassment was supreme," he recalled. "I plunged in, trusting Providence that the assembly would behave itself. But with the plunge went the determination that I would never attend another meeting until I knew something of . . . parliamentary law."[16]

---

14. Henry taught mathematics, natural philosophy, astronomy, and practical engineering; see Mehren, "Henry Martyn Robert," 798.

15. Texas General Land Office, "A 'Bulwark Against the Sea'—The Galveston Seawall," June 1, 2017, available at https://medium.com/save-texas-history/a-bulwark-against-the-sea-the-galveston-seawall-d92e2897eeaf.

16. Robert, *RRONR*, xxxvii; US Army Corps of Engineers, "Historical Vignette 038: An Engineer Brought Order to Church Meetings and Revolutionized Parliamentary Procedure," November 2001, available at https://www.usace.army.mil/About/History/Historical-Vignettes/General-History/038-Church-Meetings/.

In fact, Henry's interest in the study of voluntary group behavior cut even deeper. Henry was born in 1837 on his family's South Carolina slave plantation in the town of Robertville, named after a French-Huguenot ancestor and early settler of the Low Country Region. Henry's father, Reverend Joseph Thomas Robert, enjoyed social prominence as patriarch of one of Robertville's leading families and as the pastor of its leading church.[17] When Henry was two years old, however, his family's fortunes turned when his father's nascent antislavery views—likely formed during his studies at Brown University, in Rhode Island—prompted his ouster at Black Swamp Baptist Church and a search for a more sympathetic congregation elsewhere.[18] His search proved more arduous than expected. Over the next decade, as the slavery issue divided the country and the Baptist Church itself into warring Northern and Southern factions, Joseph, his wife, Adeline, and their seven children struggled to find a new home. They moved to Kentucky, then Ohio, then Georgia, then back to South Carolina, before returning to Ohio, in 1851, following the Reverend's decision to emancipate his family's slaves after years of anguished soul-searching. Henry's father waited out the Civil War in semi-exile teaching college mathematics and science in Iowa. He didn't return to the South until 1871 when the American Baptist Home Mission Society tapped him as the first president of the tiny theological seminary for freedmen that would eventually become

17. For the family history, see Saunders Jr. and Rogers, "Joseph Thomas Robert and the Wages of Conscience," 1–24; and Henry Petroski, "Henry Martin Robert," *American Scientist* 84, no. 2 (March 1996): 106.

18. Brown was initially endowed with proceeds from the slave trade and partly built with slave labor before emerging as a bastion of antislavery sentiment in the 1820s and 1830s. See Ruth J. Simmons, "Slavery and Justice at Brown: A Personal Reflection," in *Slavery and the University*, ed. Leslie M. Harris, James T. Campbell, and Alfred L. Brophy (Athens: University of Georgia Press, 2019), 215–23. For the full report of the Brown University Steering Committee on Slavery and Justice, see https://www.brown.edu/Research/Slavery_Justice/.

Morehouse College in Atlanta, one of the country's most revered Black-serving institutions of higher learning.[19]

Henry never revealed much about his itinerant childhood, and little is known about his education before West Point, but it seems likely that his father's travails left a lasting impression on him. Surely, Henry learned something about the courage of conviction in the face of adversity. He probably learned how important it was for contentious ideas, like his father's evolving position on slavery, to receive a fair hearing. And he also learned about the messiness of group deliberation, having witnessed congregation after congregation lose faith in his father, vote him out, only to send the family packing, again.[20]

What is certain, however, is that Henry's personal history crisscrossing the country taking in new people and places, first as a young child, then as an army engineer tasked with rationalizing society and the built environment, pushed him toward the search for an intellectual history of deliberative assemblies following that catastrophic church meeting in 1863. He took his time educating himself on the subject, collecting and poring over all the major works until he had mastered the fundamentals as well as any elected official, better even. He read and reread Thomas Jefferson's eponymous *Manual*—compiled while Jefferson was vice president (and president of the Senate) and published in 1801—to this

---

19. Joseph was mentored by Brown's president, Francis Wayland, a well-known opponent of slavery; see Saunders Jr. and Rogers, "Joseph Thomas Robert and the Wages of Conscience," 10; and https://www.brown.edu/Administration/News _Bureau/Databases/Encyclopedia/search.php?serial=W0110. On the construction of Black colleges after the Civil War, see James Anderson, *The Education of Blacks in the South, 1860–1935* (Chapel Hill: University of North Carolina Press, 1988). On the schism of the Baptist Church, see Thomas S. Kidd and Barry Hankins, *Baptists in America: A History* (New York: Oxford University Press, 2018), 117–48. Atlanta Baptist College was renamed Morehouse College in 1913.

20. On Baptist voting practices in the nineteenth century, see Saunders Jr. and Rogers, "Joseph Thomas Robert and the Wages of Conscience," 7; and Bill J. Leonard, *Baptists in America* (New York: Columbia University Press, 2005), 78–79.

day a cornerstone of parliamentary procedure in the US Congress.[21] He had also scoured Luther S. Cushing's widely used *Manual of Parliamentary Practice: Rules of Proceeding and Debate in Deliberative Assemblies*, published in 1845.[22] Cushing was the longtime Clerk of the Massachusetts House of Representatives and a renowned jurist. What piqued Henry's interest in *Cushing's Manual* was that it hadn't been written for Cushing's fellow pols but lay assemblies— ordinary people like the folks Henry rubbed elbows with at the Y, "not legislative in their character."[23]

The first edition of *Cushing's Manual* appeared shortly after the publication of French political theorist Alexis de Tocqueville's cele- brated two-volume travelogue, *Democracy in America* (1835/1840), in which he observed the American people's "art of joining" associa- tions of one kind or another for every cause imaginable, from edu- cation and temperance to poorhouses, prisons, and abolition.[24] These groups were stirred to action by the religious fervor of the Second Great Awakening and to fill the void left by the federal government's limited reach into matters of social policy. Cushing wrote his manual with all of America's "joiners" in mind.[25]

By the late 1860s, Henry thought the time had come for an up- dated users' guide to small-d democracy. His first stab at preparing a set of rules occurred while in San Francisco, in 1869, and resulted in a pithy fifteen-page pamphlet, circulated among a handful of close associates and friends, then shelved. Another five years

---

21. Thomas Jefferson, *A Manual of Parliamentary Practice* (1801; Philadelphia: Parrish, Dunning & Mears, 1853).

22. Luther S. Cushing, *Manual of Parliamentary Practice: Rules of Proceeding and Debate in Deliberative Assemblies* (1845; Boston: W. J. Reynolds & Co., 1854).

23. Quote in Cushing, *Manual of Parliamentary Practice*, 3; and, again, in Robert, *RRO*, 12.

24. Alexis de Tocqueville, *Democracy in America* (1835, 1840), trans. Arthur Gold- hammer, ed. Olivier Zunz (New York: The Library of America, 2004), 595; Johann N. Neem, *Creating a Nation of Joiners: Democracy and Civil Society in Early National Massachusetts* (Cambridge, MA: Harvard University Press, 2009).

25. Robert, *RRONR*, xxxvi. *Cushing's Manual* was updated and revised numerous times and still in print in the early twentieth century. On Cushing and his book, see Doyle, "Rules of Order," 5–6.

passed before he returned to the project in earnest in Milwaukee, in 1874, where fewer professional demands and a bitterly cold winter kept him landlocked long enough to put pen to paper.[26]

Along the way, he gathered inspiration from his personal and professional experiences navigating bureaucratic hierarchies as well as the voluntary venues of horizontal equals that absorbed him when he wasn't glued to his drafting table. Drawing on his military and engineering background, which were all about rules, and the existing works by Jefferson and Cushing, he set out to backward-map the procedural steps required to "get at the will of the assembly," as he liked to put it.[27] Although "the rules and practices of Congress" animated his thinking, formal political institutions weren't Henry's chief concern. As a career military officer sworn to defend the country and the Constitution, the less he dealt with *real* politics the better. Besides, both Jefferson's and Cushing's manuals covered that ground and were solid on the parliamentary fundamentals: the majority must rule, the minority must be heard, and fairness and cooperation must prevail if the assembly is to accomplish its business. For Henry, the real problem lay in the practical execution of these theoretical principles— of democracy in action. In his experience, too many parliamentarians cut corners; too many people didn't follow the rules. Meetings were convened absent a quorum. Steamroller tactics were permitted that flattened discussion and ended it prematurely. Indeed, often there was no real debate at all. Henry found this profoundly distressing as well as antidemocratic.

The only way to fix the problem, he concluded, was to spell out every single rule, in particular the supplementary procedures that organized debate and tended to vary dramatically from one community and association to another, known as the rules of order. "The object of Rules of Order in deliberative assemblies is to assist an assembly to accomplish the work for which it was designed, in the best possible manner," he wrote. "To do this, it is necessary to

---

26. Smedley, *Man Behind the Rules*, 11.

27. Smedley, *Great Peacemaker*, 30.

somewhat restrain the individual, as the right of an individual in any community to do what he pleases is incompatible with the best interests of the whole."[28] A logically deduced set of rules was needed to improve the efficiency and fairness of the lay community groups that had captivated Tocqueville's imagination and that Henry regarded as the heart's blood of civil society. Churches, missionary groups, women's clubs, fraternal organizations, charities, schools, colleges and universities, were some of the institutions he had in mind. These associations thrived on cooperation, created social cohesion, forged bonds of reciprocity and mutuality, and brought meaning and purpose to people's lives—not least of all his own—by transcending the muck and mire of regular politics, or so he thought. He called them "ordinary societies"—what scholars today refer to as the voluntary, or associational, sector.[29] Henry's big idea was to create uniform rules of deliberation for the sector and, if in his own roundabout way, to rehabilitate America's dilapidated political culture by focusing on the civil sphere. "Where there is no law, but every man does what is right in his own eyes," Henry warned, "there is the least of real liberty."[30]

After years of fits and starts researching and writing, Henry finally completed the manuscript in the spring of 1874 only to be stymied again. Another eighteen months passed after publishing

28. Robert, *RRO*, 4; see also Smedley, *Great Peacemaker*, 26–34.

29. For Robert's discussion of "ordinary societies," see *RRO*, 3. On the growth of voluntary associations and their role in state-building, see, for example, Morton Keller, *Affairs of State: Public Life in Late Nineteenth Century America* (Cambridge, MA.: Harvard University Press, 1977); Theda Skocpol, *Protecting Soldiers and Mothers: The Political Origins of Social Policy in the United States* (Cambridge, MA.: Belknap Press, 1995); Robert D. Putnam, *Bowling Alone: The Collapse and Revival of American Community* (New York: Simon & Schuster, 2000); Theda Skocpol, *Diminished Democracy: From Membership to Management in American Civic Life* (Norman: University of Oklahoma Press, 2003); Yoni Appelbaum, "The Guilded Age: The American Ideal of Association, 1865–1900," (PhD diss., Brandeis University, 2014); Balogh, *Associational State*; and Clemens, *Civic Gifts*. See also Olivier Zunz, *Why the American Century?* (Chicago: University of Chicago Press, 1998), 115–36.

30. Robert, *RRO*, 4.

houses in New York and Milwaukee politely but firmly turned him away. Who'd read it, they asked? Henry was convinced a lot of people would want to read *Robert's Rules of Order*. Indeed, he was so convinced a broad range of citizens were hungry to learn about the deliberative process that he decided to self-finance the first print run and give away a thousand copies of his little book with the "brick red cover" to newspaper and journal editors, and other cultural and civic elites, to prove all his doubters wrong. A handful of well-placed, positive notices and he'd have an audience and a proper publishing contract in no time.[31]

Henry's wager paid off. His savvy promotional campaign exhausted his personal stockpile of four thousand books after a few months. A real publishing contract and another printing begat more positive write-ups and even more sales.[32] Reviewers praised the low price (75 cents), compact presentation (176 pages), and simple elegance of *Robert's Rules of Order*. They commended Henry's decision to provide separate instructions for expert (Part I) and beginner parliamentarians (Part II) and for his other signature innovation, suggested by his wife, Helen, at the last minute: a handy Table of Rules Relating to Motions, located at the back of the book, right before the index, that offered users ready answers "to 200 questions of importance, without turning a leaf." Raves flowed in from all corners. "This capital little manual," asserted the *New York World*, "will displace all its predecessors as an authority on parliamentary usages." The *Pittsburgh Dispatch* summarily proclaimed that the book was "entitled to be regarded as an authority." The *Chicago Tribune* agreed: "Maj Roberts [*sic*] . . . has rendered

---

31. Smedley, *Man Behind the Rules*, 14–15.

32. For the publication history, see Margaret A. Banks, "*Robert's Rules of Order*: Editions, Reprints, and Competitors," *Law Library Journal* 80, no. 177 (1988): 177–92; and Mehren, "Henry Martyn Robert," 801. The first edition was published in February 1876 and sold out so quickly that a second edition, with 16 pages added, appeared in July of the same year. The two editions are often confused.

valuable service to a large body of people."[33] Realizing they had a surprise hit on their hands, Henry's publisher, S. C. Griggs & Company of Chicago, immediately began promoting his book as "The Best Parliamentary Manual in the English Language."[34]

Henry's user-friendly guide became a publishing sensation. In the first year, ten thousand copies sold, and by the time he put the finishing touches on *Robert's Rules of Order Revised* in 1915, the fourth and final edition on which he worked, more than a half-million were in print, with many millions more to follow.[35] Currently in its twelfth edition, and a perennial bestseller, with innumerable spinoffs available, the book's popularity was driven by the growth in voluntarism between 1870 and 1920 when the memberships of established associations rapidly expanded and a bevy of new ones emerged and federated into local, state, and national chapters. Each chapter needed a trained parliamentarian, which usually meant buying a copy or two of *Robert's Rules of Order*. White men built the biggest and most influential associations, such as the Grand Army of the Republic, which boasted over 300,000 members by the mid-1880s, but women, African Americans, and immigrants also contributed to the boom in association-building. According to one exhaustive study, half of all the largest voluntary organizations in the history of the country formed during this time period.[36]

---

33. Assorted reviews, February–April 1876, reel 7, MSS37952, Henry M. Roberts Papers, 1853–1937, Library of Congress, Washington, DC (hereafter HMRP, LOC). His surname often appeared incorrectly as *Roberts*, with an additional s. On Helen's role in the creation of the Table of Rules Relating to Motions, which was expanded and moved to the front of the book in subsequent editions, see Smedley, *Great Peacemaker*, 36.

34. Advertisements, ca. 1876, reel 7, MSS37952, HMRP, LOC.

35. Banks, *"Robert's Rules of Order,"* 179; Robert, *RRONR*, xxii. At 323 pages, *Robert's Rules of Order Revised* (Glenview, IL: Scott, Foresman and Co., 1915), was nearly double the length of the first 1876 edition.

36. Keller, *Affairs of State*; Skocpol, *Protecting Soldiers and Mothers*; Appelbaum, "Guilded Age"; Balogh, *Associational State*; Clemens, *Civic Gifts*; Stuart McConnell, *Glorious Contentment: The Grand Army of the Republic, 1865–1900* (Chapel Hill:

Henry dutifully tended to all the associational life springing up around him. His personal papers at the Library of Congress are filled with letters to and from his many devotees. Take, for example, Mary G. Hay, president of the Women's Club of New York, "an ardent student of 'Robert's Rules of Order'" who reached out to him, directly, for "a little advice."[37] Henry responded to her query and to as many others as possible, and personally attended association meetings whenever his schedule permitted, using them to fine-tune his own thinking and to make revisions to later editions.[38] He and his oldest brother Joseph ventured off in new directions with the founding of the Robert Correspondence School of Parliamentary Law. Based in Chicago, the school developed teaching tools and aids, including a book of twenty-four "easy, progressive lessons illustrating parliamentary law and practice," to teach the science of the deliberative process from a distance.[39]

Henry found plenty of individuals and organizations that were eager to learn about democratic assemblies. Early adopters included women's clubs, like the Women's Christian Temperance Union; fraternal organizations, like the Freemasons, the Knights of Pythias, and the International Order of Odd Fellows; mutual aid, theological seminaries, and religious orders, including Henry's Baptist church; veterans' groups, such as the Military Order of the Loyal Legion of the United States, and the Veterans of

University of North Carolina Press, 1997); David T. Beito, *From Mutual Aid to the Welfare State: Fraternal Societies and Social Services, 1890–1967* (Chapel Hill: University of North Carolina Press, 2000); and, for a helpful list of associations and their founding dates, with reference to Theda Skocpol, "How Americans Became Civic," in *Civic Engagement in American Democracy*, ed. Theda Skocpol and Morris P. Fiorina (Washington, DC: Brookings Institution Press, 1999), 27–80, see Putnam, *Bowling Alone*, 383–84.

37. Letter, Feb. 14, 1922, reel 3, MSS37952, HMRP, LOC.

38. Banks, "Robert's Rules of Order," 182.

39. Joseph R. Thomas, *Parliamentary Law for Schools, Colleges, Clubs, Fraternities, Etc.* (New York: Doubleday, Page & Co., 1908). Joseph served as the principal of the school. Other family members also got involved; see Plaisted, *General Henry M. Robert*, 161.

Foreign Wars; professional associations; and, in due course, labor unions, farm lobbies, garden and athletic clubs, and "assemblies and organizations of every name and nature."[40] Even politicians, the one group in which Henry had professed the least interest, thought the guide marked a significant achievement that improved on their current practices. Mayors, governors, and members of Congress, from Mississippi to New York, in a rare instance of bipartisan agreement, threw their support behind *Robert's Rules of Order*. An excited House member spoke for many of his fellow politicians when he proclaimed it an "exquisite little volume" equally well suited "to the student and to the Statesman."[41]

No organization gravitated to *Robert's Rules of Order* as forcefully as the modern university—a hub for civic training and a sprawling association of voluntary associations. Henry specifically targeted the academic sector. He gave desk copies to presidents, deans, and faculty, who received it with pleasure and a measure of relief. Joshua L. Chamberlain, president of tiny Bowdoin College, in Maine, immediately requested "40 copies for introduction in the forensic exercises of this senior class of this college." Colonel James T. Murfree, president of Howard College, a Black-serving institution, relayed that he'd been on the lookout for such a volume, and promised to use *Robert's Rules of Order* "as a regular textbook of the College." Others agreed. "I find it the most conspicuous and comprehensive embodiment of the rules observed in American assemblies, that I have ever seen," declared Erastus O. Haven, chancellor of Syracuse University. "It should be studied by all who wish to become familiar with the correct usages of public meetings."[42] The editors at the *Wisconsin Journal of Education* accurately predicted the work would become the "recognized standard" across the entire educational system.[43]

---

40. Putnam, *Bowling Alone*, 384–87; quote in Advertisements, ca. 1876, reel 7, MSS37952, HMRP, LOC.

41. Advertisements, ca. 1876, reel 7, MSS37952, HMRP, LOC.

42. Advertisements, ca. 1876, reel 7, MSS37952, HMRP, LOC.

43. Miscellaneous advertisements and letters, ca. 1876, reel 7, MSS37952, HMRP, LOC.

By offering a bottom-up guide to democratic practice that helped moderate the elitist pretensions of Gilman's expert-driven top-down university model, *Robert's Rules of Order* became the definitive guide for the rapidly growing higher education system. Between 1880 and 1920 the number of institutions grew and diversified from 811 to 1,041. Public, private, single-sex, Black-serving, and predominantly white coeducational institutions—from the tiniest liberal arts college to large-scale universities—dotted the landscape. Enrollments quintupled from 116,000 to 598,000 (and doubled again in the 1920s in what became a familiar growth pattern for the remainder of the century) as the proportion of the US population seeking advanced learning climbed from 3 to 8 percent (today, 60 percent of Americans aged twenty-five or older have some college, though only 35 percent have earned degrees). The average student body approached 600 students, but this only told part of the story, since figures ranged widely, from the miniscule to the gargantuan, with the most elite research universities having the biggest enrollments, such as Harvard with 4,650, Columbia with 8,510, and Chicago with 11,300, for example.[44]

Universities divided into colleges and schools as faculty spun off into disciplinary departments. Professors of history, English, economics, political science, psychology, anthropology, chemistry, math, engineering, and so on forged distinctive professional identities, specialized methods to prepare future experts, and national associations that standardized training to ensure consistent results. The Modern Language Association formed in 1883, the American Historical Association in 1884, and the American Economic Association in 1885. Other professional associations trailed close behind, soon enough joined by even more far-reaching national bodies, like the National Association of State Universities

---

44. Data in Thomas Snyder, ed., *120 Year of American Education: A Statistical Portrait* (Washington, DC: NCES, 1993), 75–92; and Hugh Hawkins, *Banding Together: The Rise of National Associations in Higher Education, 1887–1950* (Baltimore, MD: Johns Hopkins University Press, 1992), 2–3.

(1895), the American Association of Universities (1900), and the National College Athletic Association (1906). Elsewhere, analogous voluntary organizations of businesspeople, farmers, laborers, professional athletes, and entertainers sought the benefits of collective action in a society increasingly governed by specialization and interdependence. Universities joined this "organizational revolution" by "banding together" to influence education policy, as historian Hugh Hawkins aptly described this process of fragmentation and centralization. Some faculty who lived through the period remembered the situation a bit differently. Psychologist William James, for one, unflatteringly compared his employer, Harvard University, to a "Ph.D. Octopus"—moving every which way at once without any clear direction.[45]

Enter the administration to tame the bureaucratic beast.[46] Unknown to the old college, where fiery sermons had failed miserably to keep everyone in line, the burgeoning administrative corps relied on "conference, memorandum, and filing system," quipped historian Laurence Veysey, to paper over, as it were, the "multiplicity of cleavages" in the university's labyrinthine organization chart.[47] A dense web of deans, associates, assistants, and staff gradually assumed responsibility for everything beyond the professor's teaching and research life. This included admissions, registration, fundraising, alumni relations, and, crucially, student

45. Hawkins, *Banding Together*; Thomas Haskell, *The Emergence of Professional Social Science: The American Social Science Association and the Nineteenth-Century Crisis of Authority* (Urbana-Champaign: University of Illinois Press, 1977). James discussed in Frederick Rudolph, *The American College and University: A History* (Athens: University of Georgia Press, 1962), 397. On the bureaucratization of the university, see Veysey, *Emergence of the American University*, 263–446.

46. Tellingly, the first book on the subject was published in 1900; see Charles F. Thwing, *College Administration* (New York: The Century Co., 1900).

47. Veysey, *Emergence of the American University*, 315. On the unruliness of the nineteenth-century college, see Helen Lefkowitz Horowitz, *Campus Life: Undergraduate Cultures from the End of the Eighteenth Century to the Present* (Chicago: University of Chicago Press, 1987), 3–55.

affairs and the network of extracurricular clubs, Greek-letter societies, athletic teams, proto-professional groups, and student government organizations that served as a training ground for the
lifetime of association-building and voluntarism to come. Dart-
mouth College, University of Michigan, University of North Carolina, University of Chicago, Vanderbilt University, and even
Mr. Jefferson's University of Virginia were just some of the colleges
and universities that adopted *Robert's Rules of Order* as their sole
"parliamentary authority."[48]

In hindsight, the incorporation of *Robert's Rules of Order* occurred for self-serving, heartfelt, and practical reasons. To begin
with, the widespread adoption of the rules brought greater uniformity to parliamentary practices that contributed to the bureaucratic standardization of the emerging university model. Without
rules, Robert's and others'—governing everything from scheduling
and graduation requirements to credit hours, student conduct, and
faculty pensions—the institution would have devolved into chaos.

Next, *Robert's Rules of Order* lent the guise of formalism to an
organization anxious to grow up fast and pining for public affirma-
tion and respect. Among university leaders, faculty, and students,
the rules offered an imprimatur of solemnity and ceremony that
dovetailed with the conspicuous creation of faculty senates, academic regalia, and other rituals and governing traditions sugges-
tive of an institution that had arrived.[49]

In addition, *Robert's Rules of Order* helped the American university adjust to the demands of serving a mass democracy at the
dawn of the twentieth century. In a time of growing deference to
credentialed professionals, and with emerging ideas of a merito-
cratic order beginning to take hold in society, it was important to
provide a patina of egalitarian participation to the institution that

---

48. Advertisements, ca. 1876, reel 7, MSS37952, HMRP, LOC.

49. Veysey, *Emergence of the American University*, 302–17; Christopher P. Loss,
"Bureaucratic Tyranny: 'The Price of Structure' in the American University," *History
of Education Quarterly* 45, no. 3 (Fall 2005): 446–53.

Gilman and his fellow university builders had conceived as a repository of expertise for the modern age. The adoption of Henry's guide appeared to many to do just that.[50]

Lastly, and most important, *Robert's Rules of Order* proliferated at the moment the modern university and other voluntary associations became overtly political institutions. The "ordinary societies" that Henry imagined existing outside politics—ecclesiastical bodies, women's and African Americans' groups, mutual aid organizations, labor unions—morphed into potent political interests armed with partisan agendas focused on political and civil rights, the provision of social services, and a living wage.[51] The politics of higher education that permeated the student body and the professoriate, and that brought both parties into conflict with one another as well as the administration and board, centered on free speech and the nascent doctrine of academic freedom. Having grown tired of watching colleagues get removed for speaking truth to power, and fearful politics would swallow the campus whole, in 1900 concerned faculty formed yet another voluntary organization—the American Association of University Professors (AAUP). It took them a while to get their thoughts straight, but the AAUP finally produced a Declaration of Principles on Academic Freedom in 1915 (subsequently revised in 1940) that laid out guidelines for tenure and professorial conduct, and for (responsible) political engagement away from campus.[52]

---

50. On the various efforts to reconcile the modern university and mass democracy, see, for example, Veysey, *Emergence of the American University*, 61–68; John Higham, "The Matrix of Specialization," in *The Organization of Knowledge in Modern America, 1860–1920*, ed. Alexandra Oleson and John Voss (Baltimore, MD: Johns Hopkins University Press, 1979), 3–18; Scott Gelber, *The University and the People: Envisioning American Higher Education in an Era of Populist Protest* (Madison: University of Wisconsin Press, 2011); Joseph F. Kett, *Merit: The History of a Founding Ideal from the American Revolution to the Twenty-First Century* (Ithaca, NY: Cornell University Press, 2013), 159–91; and Jewett, *Science, Democracy, and the American University*, 117–47.

51. Balogh, *Associational State*, 1–22.

52. Matthew W. Finkin and Robert C. Post, *For the Common Good: Principles of American Academic Freedom* (New Haven, CT: Yale University Press, 2009), 11–52.

Of course, neither the adoption of *Robert's Rules of Order* nor the tacit acceptance of the doctrine of academic freedom ensured a perfectly functioning democratic institution. Theoretical rights and responsibilities meant next to nothing if they weren't jealously protected or obeyed, and soon faculty learned that procedural democracy alone was no guarantee of substantive democracy. Predictably, violations of the freedom to teach, to learn, and to pursue the truth wherever it led flared up during periods of national crisis. During the First World War, the Second World War, and on and off during the Cold War, faculty who raised questions about US involvement abroad, or drifted too far from the "vital center" of the American political tradition, ran the risk of professional and personal ruin. Some faculty were fired, others were chastened; most decided to play it safe and keep their mouths shut.[53]

Meanwhile, the student body and the extracurricular system that animated it remained bastions of white, male privilege at an institution expressly designed to perpetuate it. Until the Civil Rights Movement upended Jim Crow in the 1960s, the majority of African American students attended private segregated institutions, like Howard University in Washington, DC, or Morehouse, where Henry's father had worked, or one of the country's Black-serving public land-grant colleges, like Tennessee State University, in Nashville.[54] White women had comparatively more choices than African American students of any sex ever did. Single-sex and coordinate colleges offered two longstanding and popular options. Starting in the late nineteenth century, however, women penetrated coeducational institutions, such as the University of California and the University of Chicago. These schools were coeducational in the narrowest sense. Women students found few if any

---

53. Ellen Schrecker, *No Ivory Tower: McCarthyism and the Universities* (New York: Oxford University Press, 1986); Arthur Schlesinger Jr., *The Vital Center: The Politics of Freedom* (1949; New York: Da Capo Press, 1988).

54. Earl J. McGrath, *The Predominantly Negro Colleges and Universities in Transition* (New York: Teachers College, Columbia University, 1965).

female faculty or administrators with whom to learn from or consort. They were coerced into studying education, social work, or nursing, and other purported feminine fields of study. Their extracurricular options also remained severely limited. Socially and intellectually marginalized and sexually objectified, women were treated as second-class students, or worse.[55]

Ever since, administrators, faculty, and alumni have labored to scrub out the less seemly parts of the story—to prettify the past and take comfort in the myths of the Ivory Tower. But the fact remains that the history of the modern university is the history of the United States writ small, warts and all. In other words, the university, like our nation, had to work hard to become a juggernaut of democracy in the twentieth century. It took cooperation. It took collective action. It took deliberation, consensus-building, and, yes, a good bit of agitation and mass protest from established voluntary associations and emergent movements for minority rights to achieve the durable social and political change they wanted. It took faculty, students, and administrators working together on campus and in concert with state and federal political actors, from both sides of the aisle, to enact the policies and secure the funding to transform the higher education sector into the mass system of 4,400 institutions and 20 million students we have today.

The Second World War was the key inflection point. It changed the life of the nation and higher education forever, bringing the state and universities into partnership and extending opportunities for college access that inverted, slowly but steadily, ingrained gender and racial hierarchies. The government pumped $4 billion into research, anchored by the development of the atomic bomb, and then into the education of returning veterans under the GI Bill

---

55. Barbara Miller Solomon, *In the Company of Educated Women: A History of Women and Higher Education in America* (New Haven, CT: Yale University Press, 1986); Nancy Weiss Malkiel, *"Keep the Damned Women Out": The Struggle for Coeducation* (Princeton, NJ: Princeton University Press, 2016).

of 1944, leading to even greater investments in ideas and people later. The National Defense Education Act of 1958 launched the student-loan business. The Higher Education Act of 1965 contributed work-study and federal grants to the mix. And by the 1970s college had become a reachable goal for millions of Americans irrespective of sex or skin color—almost exactly a hundred years after the modern university and Henry Martyn Robert first joined forces to strengthen American democracy.[56]

* * *

The democratization of the US higher education system helped turn it into the "world's best."[57] How much longer it maintains that distinction will depend on how we deal with the laundry list of crises that now confront it. Over the last four decades, the consensus around higher education as a public good has withered away. Rising costs, spiraling student debt, evidence of limited learning, and chronically high dropout rates represent just a few of the sector's most daunting challenges. Add in the #MeToo and Black Lives Matter movements, another financial crisis, extreme political polarization the likes of which haven't been seen since the Gilded Age, and a global pandemic that has incited serious challenges to scientific authority (even as the development of a vaccine depended on scientific authority), and the structural and ideological sources of higher education's present struggles becomes painfully clear.

The most frustrating part is that getting a degree has become harder at the very moment that having a degree has never been more important. This is especially so for first-generation and minority students who have the most to gain from a diploma—and,

---

56. Loss, *Between Citizens and the State*, 91–213.

57. Henry Rosovsky, "Highest Education: Our Universities Are the World's Best," *New Republic* (July 13, 1987): 13.

therefore, the most to lose without one.[58] College graduates are more civically and politically engaged than their non-college-educated peers. They earn more and enjoy greater labor-market mobility. They live longer and report a higher quality of life. And they are more likely to have a significant other with a college degree, which often begets a final advantage: children from college-educated households are more likely to become college graduates themselves.[59]

In the spirit of *Robert's Rules of Order*, it seems only fitting to close with a series of questions: Is our society committed to higher learning and willing to invest in it? Do we believe in scientific and humanistic inquiry? Or have worsening budget cuts and political partisanship crippled our capacity to not only create new knowledge but to know it when we see it? What are the limits of academic freedom and free speech? Should there be any? How can we improve student access and success? What about the overproduction of graduate degrees and the adjunctification of the faculty? And are we prepared to deal honestly with our history of discrimination and white supremacy? Or will we allow it to tear us apart? In short, do we still believe in our democratic mission and are we willing to fight for it? How we call these questions will determine both the fate of the university as well as the nation itself.

Which brings us full circle to where this essay started and to a final question: Why does *Robert's Rules of Order* matter to colleges and universities today?

It matters because we won't be able to solve the problems we face unless everyone—students, faculty, administrators, elected officials, and ordinary Americans alike—plays by the same rules. The rules

---

58. See, for a recent example, Laura T. Hamilton and Kelly Nielsen, *Broke: The Racial Consequences of Underfunding Public Universities* (Chicago: University of Chicago Press, 2021).

59. On the civic, cultural, economic, and personal benefits of a college degree, see Anne Case and Angus Deaton, *Deaths of Despair and the Future of Capitalism* (Princeton, NJ: Princeton University Press, 2020), 49–61.

are simple, elegant, and proven: the majority rules; the minority must be heard and respected; cooperation and decency must prevail; and the interests of the whole must outweigh those of any individual.

At the high point of the supposed free-market order in the late nineteenth century, Henry Robert introduced his guide to ordering voluntary human behavior that stood in proud opposition to *laissez-faire*, as did many of the groups his rules served, from labor unions to reform organizations to professional associations and student clubs. So, if we want to fix our country and our higher education system, we could do no better than to follow the steps outlined in his book, remembering that effective democratic problem-solving requires collaboration, disciplined thinking, a trust in facts, sympathetic imagination, and absolute honesty from all sides. Democracy is not a natural kind. It isn't a self-correcting market that operates innately or invisibly absent the human hand. Whether on our campuses or in the larger society—from lecture halls to the Halls of Congress—real democracy takes work. That's the moral lesson at the heart of Henry Robert's book, and it remains as true today as it did in his time. We need to get busy. Time is running out.

EDITOR'S NOTE

The version of *Robert's Rules of Order* below reprints the main text of the first self-financed edition published by Henry M. Robert, in February 1876, and printed by Burdick & Armitage, in Milwaukee. Only four-thousand copies were produced. Every effort has been extended to reproduce a close facsimile of the original text, right down to the brick-red cover and gold title. And except for Robert's own alterations and corrections on page 108, only minor stylistic and grammatical changes have been made.

However, several elements in the text do require brief explanation in consideration of the reader's own experience.

The table of contents and text are formatted in the manner of a legal document: Roman numerals denote articles (e.g., Art. I); Arabic numerals denote sections (e.g., 1); and each section is marked with a silcrow, or double-s symbol (i.e., § for a single section, and §§ for multiple sections). The index headers are alphabetized, as usual, but their numeric locators refer to sections and subsections unless otherwise specified.

The text includes an elaborate notation system. Readers will encounter numerous footnotes, many of which offer Robert's thoughts on the rules and practice of Congress that had inspired him. Bracketed internal cross references with corresponding section numbers also abound, along with additional parenthetical in-text notations and asides, and, at the end of §§ 27, 35, and 42, an extended note.

The text is a product of its time. Robert used masculine pronouns and male-gendered language as a matter of course (i.e., he, his, him, himself, Chairman, Mr., Messrs., and so on). While this may contravene many readers' preference for gender-neutral language (my own included), it bears remembering that, in its day, the text's reflexive masculinity didn't scare away many female readers. From the start, women's voluntary organizations and clubs were among Robert's most ardent followers.

Finally, Robert intended his book to be "essentially a work of reference."[1] Readers should, of course, feel free to cut through the text in sequential order, front-to-back. But the more adventuresome path is to use it like the guidebook that it is, flipping between and among the table of contents and index, hopscotching from one section to another, following cross references wherever they lead, and burrowing deep into the footnotes and the Table of Rules Relating to Motions. This is where the text's hidden pleasures reveal themselves—and a main reason why *Robert's Rules of Order* remains such a fascinating work nearly 150 years after it was written.

—*CPL*

---

1. Robert, *Robert's Rules of Order Revised*, 305–6.

ROBERT'S RULES OF ORDER,

AND

WHY IT MATTERS

FOR

COLLEGES AND UNIVERSITIES

TODAY

POCKET MANUAL

OF

RULES OF ORDER

FOR

DELIBERATIVE ASSEMBLIES

PART I.

RULES OF ORDER.

A COMPENDIUM OF PARLIAMENTARY LAW, BASED UPON THE
RULES AND PRACTICE OF CONGRESS.

PART II.

ORGANIZATION AND CONDUCT OF BUSINESS.

A SIMPLE EXPLANATION OF THE METHODS OF ORGANIZING AND
CONDUCTING THE BUSINESS OF SOCIETIES, CONVENTIONS, AND
OTHER DELIBERATIVE ASSEMBLIES.

By Major HENRY M. ROBERT,

CORPS OF ENGINEERS, U.S.A.

CHICAGO: S. C. GRIGGS & COMPANY. 1876.

PREFACE.

There appears to be much needed a work on parliamentary law, based, in its general principles, upon the rules and practice of Congress, and adapted, in its details, to the use of ordinary societies. Such a work should give, not only the methods of organizing and conducting the meetings, the duties of the officers and the names of the ordinary motions, but in addition, should state in a systematic manner, in reference to each motion, its object and effect; whether it can be amended or debated; if debatable, the extent to which it opens the main question to debate; the circumstances under which it can be made, and what other motions can be made while it is pending. This Manual has been prepared with a view to supplying the above information in a condensed and systematic manner, each rule being either complete in itself, or giving references to every section that in any way qualifies it, so that a stranger to the work can refer to any special subject with safety.

To aid in quickly referring to as many as possible of the rules relating to each motion, there is placed immediately before the Index, a Table of Rules, which enables one, without turning a page, to find the answers to some two hundred questions. The Table of Rules is so arranged as to greatly assist the reader in systematizing his knowledge of parliamentary law.

The second part is a simple explanation of the common methods of conducting business in ordinary meetings, in which the motions are classified according to their uses, and those used for a similar purpose compared together. This part is expressly intended for that large class of the community, who are unfamiliar with parliamentary usages and are unwilling to devote much study to the subject, but would be glad with little labor to learn enough to enable them to take part in meetings of deliberative assemblies without fear of being out of order. The object of Rules of Order in deliberative assemblies, is to assist an assembly to accomplish the work for which it was designed, in the best possible manner. To do this, it is necessary to somewhat restrain the individual, as the right of an individual in any community to do what he pleases, is incompatible with the best interests of the whole. Where there is no law, but every man does what is right in his own eyes, there is the least of real liberty. Experience has shown the importance of definiteness in the law; and in this country, where customs are so slightly established and the published manuals of parliamentary practice so conflicting, no society should attempt to conduct business without having adopted some work upon the subject, as the authority in all cases not covered by their own rules.

It has been well said by one of the greatest of English writers on parliamentary law: "Whether these forms be in all cases the most rational or not is really not of so great importance. It is much more material that there should be a rule to go by, than what that rule is, that there may be a uniformity of proceeding in business, not subject to the caprice of the chairman, or captiousness of the members. It is very material that order, decency and regularity be preserved in a dignified public body."

H. M. R.
December, 1875.

TABLE OF CONTENTS.

Introduction.   *Page.*

  Parliamentary Law   11
  Plan of the Work   13
  " *Part I*   14
  " *Part II*   15
  Definitions   15

PART I.—RULES OF ORDER.

Art. I.—Introduction of Business.

  §1. How introduced   17
  2. Obtaining the floor   17
  3. What precedes debate on a question   18
  4. What motions to be in writing, and how they shall
    be divided   19
  5. Modification of a motion by the mover   20

Art. II.—General Classification of Motions.

  §6. Principal or Main motions   20
  7. Subsidiary or Secondary motions   20
  8. Incidental motions   21
  9. Privileged motions   21

Art. III.—Motions and their Order of Precedence.

  Privileged Motions.
  §10. To fix the time to which to adjourn   22
  11. Adjourn   22

12. Questions of privilege   24
13. Orders of the day   24
Incidental Motions.
§14. Appeal [Questions of Order]   25
15. Objection to the consideration of a question   26
16. Reading papers   27
17. Withdrawal of a motion   27
18. Suspension of the Rules   27
Subsidiary Motions.
§19. Lie on the table   28
20. Previous Question   29
21. Postpone to a certain day   30
22. Commit [or Re-commit]   31
23. Amend   32
24. Postpone indefinitely   34
Miscellaneous Motions.
§25. Filling blanks, and Nominations   34
26. Renewal of a motion   35
27. Reconsideration   35

Art. IV.—Committees and Informal Action.

§28. Committees   38
29. Forms of Reports of Committees   41
30. Reception of Reports   41
31. Adoption of Reports   42
32. Committee of the Whole   43
33. Informal consideration of a question   45

Art. V.—Debate and Decorum.

§34. Debate   46
35. Undebatable questions and those opening the main question to debate   47
36. Decorum in debate   49
37. Closing debate, methods of   50

Art. VI.—Vote.

§38. Voting, various modes of   51
39. Motions requiring more than a majority vote   54

Art. VII.—Officers and the Minutes.

§40. Chairman or President   55
41. Clerk, or Secretary, and the Minutes   57

Art. VIII.—Miscellaneous.

§42. Session   60
43. Quorum   61
44. Order of business   62
45. Amendment of the Rules of Order   64

PART II.—ORGANIZATION AND CONDUCT OF BUSINESS.

Art. IX.—Organization and Meetings.

§46. An Occasional or Mass Meeting.
    (a) Organization   65
    (b) Adoption of resolutions   66
    (c) Committee to draft resolutions '   67
    (d) Additional Officers   69
47. A Convention or Assembly of Delegates   69
48. A Permanent Society.   70
    (a) First meeting   70
    (b) Second meeting   72
49. Constitutions, By-Laws, Rules of Order and Standing Rules   74

Art. X.—Officers and Committees.

§50. President or Chairman   77
51. Secretary, or Clerk, and the Minutes   77
52. Treasurer   79
53. Committees   81

Art. XI—Introduction of Business.

§54. Introduction of Business   83

Art. XII.—Motions.

§55. Motions Classified according to their object   84
56. To Amend or Modify.
  (a) Amend   85
  (b) Commit   86
57. To Defer Action.
  (a) Postpone to a certain time   86
  (b) Lie on the table   87
58. To Suppress Debate.
  (a) Previous Question   87
  (b) An Order limiting or closing debate   88
59. To Suppress the question.
  (a) Objection to its consideration   88
  (b) Postpone indefinitely   89
  (c) Lie on the table   89
60. To Consider a question the second time,
or Reconsider   89
61. Order and Rules.
  (a) Orders of the day   91
  (b) Special orders   92
  (c) Suspension of the rules   92
  (d) Questions of order   92
  (e) Appeal   93
62. Miscellaneous.
  (a) Reading of papers   93
  (b) Withdrawal of a motion   93
  (c) Questions of privilege   93
63. To close a meeting.
  (a) Fix the time to which to adjourn   93
  (b) Adjourn   94
64. Order of Precedence of motions   94

Art. XIII.—Debate.

§65. Rules of speaking in debate   95
66. Undebatable questions and those that open the
main question to debate   96

Art. XIV.—Miscellaneous.

§67. Forms of stating and putting questions   96
68. Motions requiring a two-thirds vote for their adoption   97
69. Unfinished business   98
70. Session   98
71. Quorum   99
72. Order of Business   99
73. Amendment of Constitutions, By-Laws and Rules
    of Order   100

Legal Rights of Deliberative Assemblies   100

Table of Rules Relating to Motions   103

Miscellaneous Rules   106

Additions and Corrections   108

Index   109

INTRODUCTION

Parliamentary Law.

Parliamentary Law refers originally to the customs and rules of conducting business in the English Parliament; and thence to the customs and rules of our own legislative assemblies. In England these customs and usages of Parliament form a part of the unwritten law of the land, and in our own legislative bodies they are of authority in all cases where they do not conflict with existing rules or precedents.

But as a people we have not the respect which the English have for customs and precedents, and are always ready for innovations which we think are improvements, and hence changes have been and are being constantly made in the written rules which our legislative bodies have found best to adopt. As each house adopts its own rules, it results that the two houses of the same legislature do not always agree in their practice; even in Congress the order of precedence of motions is not the same in both houses, and the Previous Question is admitted in the House of Representatives, but not in the Senate. As a consequence of this, the exact method of conducting business in any particular legislative body is to be obtained only from the Legislative Manual of that body.

The vast number of societies, political, literary, scientific, benevolent and religious, formed all over the land, though not legislative, are still deliberative in their character, and must have some system of conducting business, and some rules to govern their proceedings, and are necessarily subject to the common parliamentary law where it does not conflict with their own special rules. But as their knowledge of parliamentary law has been obtained from the usages in this country, rather than from the customs of Parliament, it has resulted that these societies have followed the customs of our own legislative bodies, and our people have thus been educated under a system of parliamentary law which is peculiar to this country, and yet so well established as to supersede the English parliamentary law as the common law of ordinary deliberative assemblies.

The practice of the National House of Representatives should have the same force in this country as the usages of the House of Commons have in England, in determining the general principles of the common parliamentary law of the land; but it does not follow that in every matter of detail the rules of Congress can be appealed to as the common law governing every deliberative assembly. In these matters of detail, the rules of each House of Congress are adapted to their own peculiar wants, and are of no force whatever in other assemblies.

But upon all great parliamentary questions, such as what motions can be made, what is their order of precedence, which can be debated, what is their effect, etc., the common law of the land is settled by the practice of the U.S. House of Representatives, and not by that of the English Parliament, the U.S. Senate, or any other body.

While in extreme cases there is no difficulty in deciding the question as to whether the practice of Congress determines the common parliamentary law, yet between these extremes there must necessarily be a large number of doubtful cases upon which there would be great difference of opinion, and to avoid the serious difficulties always arising from a lack of definiteness in the law, every deliberative assembly should imitate our legislative bodies in adopting Rules of Order for the conduct of their business.*

---

* Where the practice of Congress differs from that of Parliament upon a material point, the common law of this country follows the practice of Congress. Thus in every American deliberative assembly having no rules for conducting business, the motion to adjourn would be decided to be undebatable, as in Congress, the English parliamentary law to the contrary notwithstanding; so if the Previous Question were negatived, the debate upon the subject would continue as in Congress, whereas in Parliament the subject would be immediately dismissed; so too the Previous

Plan of the Work.

This Manual is prepared to partially meet this want in deliberative assemblies that are not legislative in their character. It has been made sufficiently complete to answer for the rules of an assembly, until they see fit to adopt special rules conflicting with and superseding any of its rules of detail, such as the Order of Business [§ 44], etc. Even in matters of detail the practice of Congress is followed, wherever it is not manifestly unsuited to ordinary

---

Question could be moved when there was before the assembly a motion either to amend, to commit, or to postpone definitely or indefinitely, just as in Congress, notwithstanding that, according to English parliamentary law, the Previous Question could not be moved under such circumstances.

When the rules of the two Houses of Congress conflict, the H.R. rules are of greater authority than those of the Senate in determining the parliamentary law of the country, just as the practice of the House of Commons, and not the House of Lords, determines the parliamentary law of England. For instance, though the Senate rules do not allow the motion for the Previous Question, and make the motion to postpone indefinitely take precedence of every other subsidiary motion [§ 7] except to lie on the table, yet the parliamentary law of the land follows the practice of the House of Representatives, in recognizing the Previous Question as a legitimate motion, and assigning to the very lowest rank the motion to postpone indefinitely.

But in matters of detail, the rules of the House of Representatives are adapted to the peculiar wants of that body, and are of no authority in any other assembly. No one for instance would accept the following H.R. rules as common parliamentary law in this country: That the chairman, in case of disorderly conduct, would have the power to order the galleries to be cleared; that the ballot could not be used in electing the officers of an assembly; that any fifteen members would be authorized to compel the attendance of absent members and make them pay the expenses of the messengers sent after them; that all committees not appointed by the Chair would have to be appointed by ballot, and if the required number were not elected by a majority vote, then a second ballot must be taken in which a plurality of votes would prevail; that each member would be limited in debate upon any question, to one hour; that a day's notice must be given of the introduction of a bill, and that before its passage it must be read three times, and that without the special order of the assembly it cannot be read twice the same day. These examples are sufficient to show the absurdity of the idea that the rules of Congress in all things determine the common parliamentary law.

assemblies, and in such cases, in Part I, there will be found, in a foot note, the Congressional practice. In the important matters referred to above, in which the practice of the House of Representatives settles the common parliamentary law of the country, this Manual strictly conforms to such practice.*

Part I contains a set of Rules of Order systematically arranged, as shown in the Table of Contents. Each one of the forty-five sections is complete in itself, so that no one unfamiliar with the work can be misled in examining any particular subject. Cross references are freely used to save repeating from other sections, and by this means the reader, without using the index, is referred to everything in the Rules of Order that has any bearing upon the subject he is investigating. The references are by sections, and for convenience the numbers of the sections are placed at the top of each page. The motions are arranged under the usual classes, in their order of rank, but in the index under the word motion will be found an alphabetical list of all the motions generally used. In reference to each motion there is stated:

---

* On account of the party lines being so strictly drawn in Congress, no such thing as harmony of action is possible, and it has been found best to give a bare majority in the House of Representatives (but not in the Senate) the power to take final action upon a question without allowing of any discussion. In ordinary societies more regard should be paid to the rights of the minority, and a two-thirds vote be required, as in this Manual [§ 39], for sustaining an objection to the introduction of a question, or for adopting a motion for the Previous Question, or for adopting an order closing or limiting debate. In this respect the policy of the Pocket Manual is a mean between those of the House and Senate. But some societies will doubtless find it advantageous to follow the practice of the H.R., and others will prefer that of the Senate. It requires a majority, according to the Pocket Manual, to order the yeas and nays, which is doubtless best in the majority of assemblies; but in all bodies in which the members are responsible to their constituents, a much smaller number should have this power. In Congress it requires but a one-fifth vote, and in some bodies a single member can require a vote to be taken by yeas and nays.

Any society adopting this Manual, should make its rules govern them in all cases to which they are applicable, and in which they are not inconsistent with the By-Laws and Rules of Order of the society. Their own rules should include all of the cases where it is desirable to vary from the rules in the Manual, and especially should provide for a Quorum [§ 43], and an Order of Business [§ 44], as suggested in these rules.

(1) Of what motions *it takes precedence* (that is, what motions may, be pending, and yet it be in order to make this motion).

(2) To what motions it *yields* (that is, what motions may be made while this motion is pending).

(3) Whether it is *debatable* or not.

(4) Whether it can be *amended* or not.

(5) In case the motion can have no subsidiary motion *applied* to it, the fact is stated [see Adjourn, § 11, for an example: the meaning is, that the particular motion to adjourn, for example, cannot be laid on the table, postponed, committed or amended].

(6) The *effect* of the motion if adopted.

(7) The *form of stating the question* when peculiar, and whatever other information is necessary to enable one to understand the question.

Part II. While the second part covers the entire ground of the first part, it does so in a much simpler manner, being intended for those who have no acquaintance with the usages of deliberative assemblies. It also explains the method of organizing an assembly or society, and conducting a meeting. The motions are treated on an entirely different plan, being classified according to the objects for which they are used, and those of each class compared together so that the reader may obtain the best motion for the accomplishment of any given object. It omits the complications of parliamentary law, and has but few references to the rules of Congress, or those in this Manual. In order to make it complete in itself, it was necessary to repeat a few pages from the first part.

DEFINITIONS.

In addition to the terms defined above (*taking precedence of, yielding to* and *applying to*), there are other terms that are liable to be misunderstood, to which attention should he called.

Meeting and *Session.*—In this Manual the term "meeting" is used to denote an assembling together of the members of a deliberative assembly for any length of time, during which there is no separation of the members by adjournment. An adjournment to meet again at some other time, even the same day, terminates the meeting, but not the session, which latter includes all the adjourned meetings. The next meeting, in this case, would be an "adjourned meeting" of the same session.

A "meeting" of an assembly is terminated by a temporary adjournment; a "session" of an assembly ends with an adjournment without day, and may consist of many meetings [see Session, § 42].

Previous Question—This term is frequently understood to refer to the question previously under consideration. As used in this country it is equivalent to a motion to "Stop debate, and proceed to voting on all the questions before the assembly," with certain exceptions, where it affects only one motion (as to postpone, to reconsider and an appeal; see § 20 for a full explanation).

Shall the Question be Considered (or discussed)? This question, which is put as soon as a subject is brought before an assembly, if any member "objects to its consideration" (or "discussion," or "introduction"), is not intended to merely cut off debate, but to prevent the question from coming before the assembly for its action. If decided by a two-thirds vote in the negative, the question is removed from before the assembly immediately [see § 15].

Whenever the word "assembly," which is used throughout these rules, occurs in forms of motions (as in Appeals, § 14), it is better to replace it by the special term used to designate the particular assembly; as for instance, "Society," or "Convention," or "Board." The term "Congress," when used in this Manual, refers to the House of Representatives of the U.S.

PART I.

Rules of Order.

Art. I. Introduction of Business.

[§§ 1–5.]

1. All business should be brought before the assembly by a motion of a member, or by the presentation of a communication to the assembly. It is not usual, however, to make a motion to receive the reports of committees [§ 30] or communications to the assembly; and in many other cases in the ordinary routine of business, the formality of a motion is dispensed with; but should any member object, a regular motion becomes necessary.

2. Before a member can make a motion or address the assembly upon any question, it is necessary that he **obtain the floor**; that is, he must rise and address the presiding officer by his title, thus: "Mr. Chairman" [§ 34], who will then announce the member's name. Where two or more rise at the same time the Chairman must decide who is entitled to the floor, which he does by announcing that member's name. From this decision, however, an appeal [§ 14] can be taken; though if there is any doubt as to who is entitled to the floor, the Chairman can at the first allow the assembly to decide the question by a vote—the one getting the largest vote being entitled to the floor.

The member upon whose motion the subject under discussion was brought before the assembly (or, in case of a committee's report, the one who presented the report) is entitled to be recognized as having the floor (if he has not already had it during that discussion), notwithstanding another member may have first risen and addressed the Chair. If the Chairman rise to speak before the floor has been assigned to any one, it is the duty of a member who may have previously risen to take his seat. [See Decorum in Debate, § 36.]

When a member has obtained the floor, he cannot be cut off from addressing the assembly, nor be interrupted in this speech by a motion to adjourn, or for any purpose, by either the Chairman or any member, except (a) to have entered on the minutes a motion to reconsider [§ 27]; (b) by a call to order [§ 14]; (c) by an objection to the consideration of the question [§ 15]; or (d) by a call for the orders of the day [§ 13].*

In such cases the member when he arises and addresses the Chair should state at once for what purpose he rises, as, for instance, that he "rises to a point of order." A call for an adjournment, or for the question, by members in their seats, is not a motion; as no motion can be made, without rising and addressing, the Chair, and being announced by the presiding officer. Such calls for the question are themselves breaches of order, and do not prevent the speaker from going on if he pleases.

3. Before any subject is open to debate [§ 34] it is necessary, first, that a motion he made; second, that it be seconded, (see exceptions below); and third, that it be stated by the presiding officer. When the motion is in writing it shall be handed to the Chairman, and read before it is debated.

This does not prevent suggestions of alterations, before the question is stated by the presiding officer. To the contrary, much time may be saved by such informal remarks; which, however, must never be allowed to run into debate. The member who offers the motion, until it has been stated by the presiding officer, can modify his motion, or even withdraw it entirely; after it is stated he can do neither, without the consent of the assembly [see §§ 5 and 17]. When the mover modifies his motion, the one who seconded it can withdraw his second.

Exceptions: A call for the order of the day, a question of order (though not an appeal), or an objection to the consideration of a

---

* See note to § 61.

question [§§ 13, 14, 15], does not have to be seconded; and many questions of routine are not seconded or even made; the presiding officer merely announcing that, if no objection is made, such will be considered the action of the assembly.

4. All Principal Motions [§ 6], Amendments and Instructions to Committees, should be in writing, if required by the presiding officer. Although a question is complicated, and capable of being made into several questions, no one member (without there is a special rule allowing it) can insist upon its being divided; his resource is to move that the question be divided, specifying in his motion how it is to be divided. Any one else can move as an amendment to this, to divide it differently.

This *Division of a Question* is really an amendment [§ 23], and subject to the same rules. Instead of moving a division of the question, the same result can be usually attained by moving some other form of an amendment. When the question is divided, each separate question must be a proper one for the assembly to act upon, even if none of the others were adopted. Thus, a motion to "commit with instructions," is indivisible, because if divided, and the motion to commit should fail, then the other motion to instruct the committee would be improper, as there would be no committee to instruct.* The motion to "strike out certain words and insert others," is indivisible, as it is strictly one proposition.

---

* The 46th Rule of the House of Representatives requires the division of a question on the demand of one member, provided "it comprehends propositions in substance so distinct that one being taken away, a substantive proposition shall remain for the decision of the House." But this does not allow a division so as to have a vote on separate items or names. The 121st Rule expressly provides that on the demand of one-fifth of the members a separate vote shall be taken on such items separately, and others collectively, as shall be specified in the call, in the case of a bill making appropriations for internal improvements. But this right to divide a question into items extends to no case but the one specified. The common parliamentary law allows of no division except when the assembly orders it, and in ordinary assemblies this rule will be found to give less trouble than the Congressional one.

5. After a question has been stated by the presiding officer, it is in the possession of the assembly for debate; the mover cannot withdraw or modify it, if any one objects, except by obtaining leave from the assembly [§ 17], or by moving an amendment.

ART. II. GENERAL CLASSIFICATION OF MOTIONS.

[§§ 6–9.]

6. **A Principal or Main Question or Motion**, is a motion made to bring before the assembly, for its consideration, any particular subject. No Principal Motion can be made when any other question is before the assembly. It takes precedence of nothing, and yields to all Privileged, Incidental and Subsidiary Questions [§§ 7, 8, 9].

7. **Subsidiary or Secondary Questions or Motions** relate to a Principal Motion, and enable the assembly to dispose of it in the most appropriate manner. These motions take precedence of the Principal Question, and must be decided before the Principal Question can be acted upon. They yield to Privileged and Incidental Questions [§§ 8, 9], and are as follows (being arranged in their order of precedence among themselves):

Lie on the Table... § 19.
The Previous Question.. § 20.
Postpone to a Certain Day... § 21.
Commit... § 22.
Amend.. § 23.
Postpone Indefinitely... § 24.

Any of these motions (except Amend) can be made when one of a lower order is pending, but none can supersede one of a higher order. They cannot be applied* to one another except in the

---

* See Plan of Work and Definitions, in Introduction, for explanation of some of these technical terms.

following cases: (a) the Previous Question applies to the motion to Postpone, without affecting the principal motion, and can, if specified, be applied to a pending amendment [§ 20]; (b) the motions to Postpone to a certain day, and to Commit, can be amended; and (c) a motion to Amend the minutes can be laid on the table without carrying the minutes with it [§ 19].

8. **Incidental Questions** are such as arise out of other questions, and, consequently, take precedence of, and are to be decided before, the questions which give rise to them. They yield to Privileged Questions [§ 9], and cannot be amended. Excepting an Appeal, they are undebatable; an Appeal is debatable or not, according to circumstances, as shown in § 14. They are as follows:

Appeal (or Questions of Order) ....§ 14.
Objection to the Consideration of a Question......................§ 15.
The Reading of Papers...§ 16.
Leave to Withdraw a Motion..§ 17.
Suspension of the Rules ....§ 18.

9. **Privileged Questions** are such as, on account of their importance, take precedence over all other questions whatever, and on account of this very privilege they are undebatable [§ 35], excepting when relating to the rights of the assembly or its members, as otherwise they could be made use of so as to seriously interrupt business. They are as follows (being arranged in their order of precedence among themselves):

To Fix the Time to which the Assembly shall Adjourn ....§ 10.
Adjourn..§ 11.
Questions relating to the Rights and Privileges of the
    Assembly or any of its Members.....................................§ 12.
Call for the Orders of the Day ....§ 13.

ART. III. MOTIONS AND THEIR
ORDER OF PRECEDENCE.*

[§§ 10–27.]

Privileged Motions.

[§§ 10–13. SEE § 9.]

10. To Fix the Time to which the Assembly shall Adjourn.
This motion takes precedence of all others, and is in order even
after the assembly has voted to adjourn, provided the Chairman
has not announced the result of the vote. If made when another
question is before the assembly, it is undebatable [§ 35]; it can be
amended by altering the time. If made when no other question is
before the assembly, it stands as any other principal motion, and
is debatable.† The *Form* of this motion is, "When this assembly
adjourns, it adjourns to meet at such a time."

11. To Adjourn. This motion (when unqualified) takes precedence of all others, except to "fix the time to which to adjourn," to
which it yields. It is not debatable, and cannot be amended, or
have any other subsidiary motion [§ 7] applied to it. If qualified in
any way it loses its privileged character, and stands as any other
principal motion. The motion to adjourn can be repeated if there
has been any intervening business, though it be simply progress in
debate [§ 26]. When a committee is through with any business
referred to it, and prepared to report, instead of adjourning, a motion should be made "to rise," which motion, in committee, has
the same privileges as to adjourn in the assembly [§ 32].

---

* For a list of all the ordinary motions, arranged in their order of precedence, see
§ 64. All the Privileged and Subsidiary ones in this Article are so arranged.

† In ordinary societies it is better to follow the common parliamentary law, and
permit this question to be introduced as a principal question, when it can be debated
and suppressed [§ 58, 59] like other questions. In Congress, it is never debatable, and
has entirely superseded the unprivileged and inferior motion to "adjourn to a particular time."

The *Effect upon Unfinished Business* of an adjournment is as follows* [see Session, § 42]:

(a) When it does not close the session, the business interrupted by the adjournment is the first in order after the reading of the minutes at the next meeting, and is treated the same as if there had been no adjournment; an adjourned meeting being legally the continuation of the meeting of which it is an adjournment.

(b) When it closes a session in an assembly which has more than one regular session each year, then the unfinished business is taken up at the next succeeding session previous to new business, and treated the same as if there had been no adjournment [see § 44, for its place in the order of business]. Provided, that, in a body elected for a definite time (as a board of directors elected for one year), unfinished business falls to the ground with the expiration of the term for which the board or any portion of them were elected.

(c) When the adjournment closes a session in an assembly which does not meet more frequently than once a year, or when the assembly is an elective body, and this session ends the term of a portion of the members, the adjournment shall put an end to all business unfinished at the close of the session. The business can be introduced at the next session, the same as if it had never been before the assembly.

---

* "After six days from the commencement of a second or subsequent session of any Congress, all bills, resolutions and reports which originated in the House, and at the close of the next preceding session remained undetermined, shall be resumed, and acted on in the same manner as if an adjournment had not taken place." Rule 136, H.R. Any ordinary society that meets as seldom as once each year, is apt to be composed of as different membership at its successive meetings, as any two successive Congresses, and only trouble would result from allowing unfinished business to hold over to the next yearly meeting.

12. **Questions of Privilege.** Questions relating to the rights and privileges of the assembly, or any of its members, take precedence of all other questions, except the two preceding, to which they yield. The Previous Question [§ 20] can be applied to these, as to all other debatable questions.

13. **Orders of the Day.** A call for the Orders of the Day takes precedence of every other motion, excepting to Reconsider [§ 27], and the three preceding, to which latter three it yields, and is not debatable, nor can it be amended. It does not require to be seconded.

When one or more subjects have been assigned to a particular day or hour, they become the Orders of the Day for that day or hour, and they cannot be considered before that time, except by a two-thirds vote [§ 39]. And when that day or hour arrives, if called up, they take precedence of all but the three preceding questions [§§ 10, 11, 12]. Instead of considering them, the assembly may appoint another time for their consideration. If not taken up on the day specified, the order falls to the ground.

When the Orders of the Day are taken up, it is necessary to take up the separate questions in their exact order, the one first assigned to the day or hour, taking precedence of one afterwards assigned to the same day or hour. (A motion to take up a particular part of the Orders of the Day, or a certain question, is not a privileged motion). Any of the subjects, when taken up, instead of being then considered, can be assigned to some other time.

The *Form* of this question, as put by the Chair when the proper time arrives, or on the call of a member, is, "Shall the Order of the Day be taken up?" or, "Will the assembly now proceed with the Orders of the Day?"

The *Effect* of an *affirmative vote* on a call for the Orders of the Day, is to remove the question under consideration from before the assembly, the same as if it had been interrupted by an adjournment [§ 11].

The *Effect* of a *negative vote* is to dispense with the orders merely so far as they interfere with the consideration of the question then before the assembly.

Incidental Motions.

[§§ 14–18; SEE § 8]

14. **Appeal [Questions of Order].** A Question of Order takes precedence of the question giving rise to it, and must be decided by the presiding officer without debate. If a member objects to the decision, he says, "I appeal from the decision of the Chair." If the Appeal is seconded, the Chairman immediately states the question as follows: "Shall the decision of the Chair stand as the judgement of the assembly?"* This Appeal yields to Privileged Questions [§ 9]. It cannot be amended; it cannot be debated when it relates simply to indecorum [§ 36], or to transgressions of the rules of speaking, or to the priority of business, or if it is made while the previous question [§ 20] is pending. When debatable, no member is allowed to speak but once, and whether debatable or not, the presiding officer, without leaving the Chair, can state the reasons upon which he bases his decision. The motions to Lie on the Table [§ 19], or for the Previous Question [§ 20], can be applied to an Appeal, when it is debatable, and when adopted they affect nothing but the Appeal. The vote on an Appeal may also be reconsidered [§ 27]. An Appeal is not in order when another Appeal is pending.

It is the duty of the presiding officer to enforce the rules and orders of the assembly, without debate or delay. It is also the right of every member, who notices a breach of a rule to insist upon its enforcement. In such cases he shall rise from his seat, and say, "Mr. Chairman, I rise to a point of order." The speaker should immediately take his seat, and the Chairman requests the member to state his point of order, which he does, and resumes his seat. The Chair decides the point, and then, if no appeal is taken, permits the first member to resume his speech. If the member's remarks are decided to be improper, and any one objects to his continuing his speech, he cannot continue it without a vote of the assembly to that effect. Instead of the method just described, it is usual,

---

* The word Assembly can be replaced by Society, Convention, Board, etc., according to the name of the organization.

when it is simply a case of improper language used in debate, for a member to say, "I call the gentleman to order;" the Chairman decides whether the speaker is in or out of order, and proceeds as before. The Chairman can ask the advice of members when he has to decide questions of order, but the advice must be given sitting, to avoid the appearance of debate; or the Chair, when unable to decide the question, may at once submit it to the assembly. The effect of laying an appeal on the table, is to sustain, at least for the time, the decision of the Chair, and does not carry to the table the question which gave rise to the question of order.

15. **Objection to the Consideration of a Question.** An objection can be made to any principal motion [§ 6], but only when it is first introduced, before it has been debated. It is similar to a question of order [§ 14,] in that it can be made while another member has the floor, and does not require a second; and as the Chairman can call a member to order, so can he put this question if he deems it necessary, upon his own responsibility. It cannot be debated [§ 35] or have any subsidiary motion [§ 7] applied to it. When a motion is made and any member "objects to its consideration," the Chairman shall immediately put the question, "Will the assembly consider it?" or, "Shall the question be considered" [or discussed]? If decided in the negative by a two-thirds vote [§ 39], the whole matter is dismissed for that session [§ 42]; otherwise the discussion continues as if this question had never been made.

The *Object* of this motion is not to cut off debate (for which other motions are provided, see § 37), but to enable the assembly to avoid altogether any question which it may deem irrelevant, unprofitable or contentious.*

---

* In Congress, the introduction of such questions could be temporarily prevented by a majority vote under the 41st Rule of the House of Representatives, which is as follows: "Where any motion or proposition is made, the question, 'Will the House now consider it?' shall not be put unless it is demanded by some member, or is deemed necessary by the Speaker." The English use the "Previous Question," for a similar purpose [see note to § 20].

16. **Reading Papers.** [For the order of precedence, see § 8.] Where papers are laid before the assembly, every member has a right to have them once read before he can be compelled to vote on them, and whenever a member asks for the reading of any such paper, evidently for information, and not for delay, the Chair should direct it to be read, if no one objects. But a member has not the right to have anything read (excepting stated above) without getting permission from the assembly.

17. **Withdrawal of a Motion.** [For order of precedence, see § 8.] When a question is before the assembly and the mover wishes to withdraw or modify it, or substitute a different one in its place, if no one objects, the presiding officer grants the permission; if any objection is made, it will be necessary to obtain leave to withdraw, etc., on a motion for that purpose. This motion cannot be debated or amended. When a motion is withdrawn, the effect is the same as if it had never been made.*

18. **Suspension of the Rules.** [For the order of precedence, see § 8.] This motion is not debatable, and cannot be amended, nor can any subsidiary [§ 7] motion be applied to it, nor a vote on it be reconsidered [§ 27], nor a motion to suspend the rules for the same purpose be renewed [§ 26] at the same meeting, though it may be renewed after an adjournment, though the next meeting be held the same day.† The rules of the assembly shall not be suspended except for a definite purpose, and by a two-thirds vote.

The question of consideration is seldom raised in Congress, but in assemblies with very short sessions, where but few questions can or should be considered, it seems a necessity that two-thirds of the assembly should be able to instantly throw out a question they do not wish to consider. The more common form, in ordinary societies, of putting this question, is, "Shall the question be discussed?" The form to which preference is given in the rule conforms more to the Congressional one, and is less liable to be misunderstood.

* In Congress, a motion may be withdrawn by the mover, before a decision or amendment [Rule 40, H.R.]. Nothing would be gained in ordinary societies by varying from the common law as stated above.

† In Congress, it cannot be renewed the same day.

The *Form* of this motion is, to "suspend the rules which interfere with," etc., specifying the object of the suspension.

Subsidiary Motions.

[§§ 19–24; SEE § 7.]

19. **To Lie on the Table.** This motion takes precedence of all other Subsidiary Questions [§ 7], and yields to any Privileged [§ 9] or Incidental [§ 8] Question. It is not debatable, and cannot be amended or have any other subsidiary motion [§ 7] applied to it. It removes the subject from consideration till the assembly vote to take it from the table.

The *Form* of this motion is, "I move that the question lie on the table," or, "that it be laid on the table," or, "to lay the question on the table." When it is desired to take the question up again, a motion is made, either "to take the question from the table," or "to now consider such and such a question;" which motion is undebatable, and cannot have any subsidiary motion applied to it.

The *Object* of this motion is to postpone the subject in such a way, that at any time it can be taken up, either at the same or some future meeting, which could not be accomplished by a motion to postpone, either definitely or indefinitely. It is also frequently used to suppress a question [§ 59], which it does, provided a majority vote can never be obtained to take it from the table during that session [§ 42].

The *Effect* of this motion is in general to place on the table everything that adheres to the subject; so that if an amendment be ordered to lie on the table, the subject which it is proposed to amend, goes there with it. The following cases are exceptional: (a) An appeal [§ 14] being laid on the table, has the effect of sustaining, at least for the time, the decision of the Chair, and does not carry the original subject to the table. (b) So when a motion to reconsider [§ 27] a question is laid on the table, the original question is left where it was before the reconsideration was moved.

(c) An amendment to the minutes being laid on the table does not carry the minutes with it.

Even after the ordering of the Previous Question up to the moment of taking the last vote under it, it is in order to lay upon the table the questions still before the assembly.

20. **The Previous Question*** takes precedence of every debatable question [§ 35], and yields to Privileged [§ 9] and Incidental [§ 8] questions, and to the motion to Lie on the table [§ 19]. It is not debatable, and cannot be amended or have any other Subsidiary [§ 7] motion applied to it. It shall require a two-thirds vote for its adoption.

When a member calls for the previous question, and the call is seconded, the presiding officer must immediately put the question: "Shall the main question be now put?" If adopted, the member who introduced the pending measure still has the right to close the debate [§ 34]; after which the presiding officer, without allowing further discussion, shall put to vote the questions before the assembly, in their order of precedence, till the main question, with all its subsidiary and incidental questions, is disposed of (see the exceptions below). If it fails, the discussion continues as if this motion had not been made.

-----

* The Previous Question is a technical name for this motion, conveying a wrong impression of its import, as it has nothing to do with the subject previously under consideration. To demand the previous question is equivalent in effect to moving "That debate now cease, and the assembly immediately proceed to vote on the questions before it," (the exceptions are stated above). The English Previous Question is an entirely different one from ours, and is used for a different purpose. In the English Parliament it is moved by the enemies of a measure, who then vote in the negative, and thus prevent for the day, the consideration of the main question, (which in this country could be accomplished by "objecting to the consideration of the question" [§ 15], if the objection were sustained). In our Congress, it is moved by the friends of a measure, who vote in the affirmative with a view to cutting off debate and immediately bringing the assembly to a vote on the questions before it. The rules in the two cases are as different as the objects of the motions. It requires only a majority vote for its adoption in the House of Representatives, and is not allowed in the United States Senate.

The previous question can be moved on a pending amendment, and if adopted, debate is closed on the amendment only. After the amendment is voted on, the main question is again open to debate and amendments. [In this case the form of the question would be similar to this: "Shall the amendment be now put to the question?"] The Object of this motion is to bring the assembly to a vote on the question before it without further debate. In ordinary assemblies it is rarely expedient to deprive a large minority of the right of debate, and yet two-thirds of the members should have the right to close the debate when they think it best.

It applies to questions of privilege [§ 12] as well as any other debatable questions. It is allowable for a member to submit a resolution and at the same time move the previous question thereon.

To *Illustrate the Effect* of this motion, suppose it is adopted when we have before the assembly, (a) the main question; (b) an amendment; (c) a motion to commit; (d) a motion to amend the last motion by giving the committee instructions. The previous question being carried, the presiding officer would immediately put the question on the last motion (d); then on the motion to commit, (c); and if this is adopted, of course the subject is referred to the committee and disposed of for the present; but if it fails, the amendment (b) is put, and finally the main question.

Exceptions: If the Previous Question is carried while a motion to Postpone is pending, its effect is only to bring the assembly to a vote on that motion; if it is voted not to postpone, the subject is again open for debate. So if an Appeal [§ 14] or a motion to Reconsider [§ 27] is pending when the Previous Question is ordered, it applies only to them and is exhausted by the vote on them.

An affirmative vote on the motion to Commit [§ 22] exhausts the Previous Question, and if the vote is reconsidered, it is divested of the Previous Question.

[For other methods of closing debate, see § 37 and § 58.]

21. **To Postpone to a Certain Day.** This motion takes precedence of a motion to Commit, or Amend, or Indefinitely Postpone, and yields to any Privileged [§ 9] or Incidental [§ 8] question, and

to the motion to Lie on the Table, or for the Previous Question. It can be amended by altering the time, and the Previous Question can be applied to it without affecting any other motions pending. It allows of very limited debate [§ 35], and that must not go into the merits of the subject matter any further than is necessary to enable the assembly to judge the propriety of the postponement.

The *Effect* of this motion is to postpone the entire subject to the time specified, until which time it cannot be taken up except by a two-thirds vote [§ 13]. When that time arrives it is entitled to be taken up in preference to every thing except Privileged questions. Where several questions are postponed to different times and are not reached then, they shall be considered in the order of the times to which they were postponed. It is not in order to postpone to a time beyond that session [§ 42] of the assembly, except* to the day of the next session when it comes up with the unfinished business, and consequently takes precedence of new business [§ 44]. If it is desired to hold an adjourned meeting to consider a special subject, the time to which the assembly shall adjourn [§ 10] should be first fixed before making the motion to postpone the subject to that day.

22. **To Commit** [or Recommit as it is called when the subject has been previously committed]. This motion takes precedence of the motions to Amend or Indefinitely Postpone, and yields to any Privileged [§ 9] or Incidental [§ 8] Question, and also to the motion to Lie on the Table, or for the Previous Question, or to Postpone to a certain day. It can be amended by altering the committee, or giving it instructions. It is debatable, and opens to debate [§ 35] the merits of the question it is proposed to commit.

The *Form* of this motion is "to refer the subject to a committee." When different committees are proposed they should he voted in the following order: (1) Committee the whole [§ 32], (2) a standing committee, and (3) a special (or select) committee. The number of a committee is usually decided without the formality of a

---

* In Congress a motion cannot be postponed to the next session, but it is customary in ordinary societies.

motion, as in filling blanks [§ 25]: the Chairman asks "of how many shall the committee consist?" and a question is then put upon each number suggested, beginning with the largest. The number and kind of the committee need not be decided till after it has been voted to refer the subject to a committee. If the committee is a select one, and the motion does not include the method of appointing it, and there is no standing rule on the subject, the Chairman inquires how the committee shall be appointed, and this is usually decided informally. Sometimes the Chair "appoints," in which case he names the members of the committee and no vote is taken upon them; or the committee is "nominated" either by the Chair or members of the assembly (no member nominating more than one except by general consent), and then they are all voted upon together, except where more nominations are made than the number of the committee, when they shall be voted upon singly.

Where a committee is one for action (a committee of arrangements for holding a public meeting, for example), it should generally be small, and no one placed upon it who is not favorable to the proposed action; and if any such should be appointed he should ask to be excused. But when the committee is for deliberation or investigation, it is of the utmost importance that all parties be represented on it, so that in committee the fullest discussion may take place, and thus diminish the chances of unpleasant debates in the assembly.

In ordinary assemblies, by judicious appointment of committees, debates upon delicate and troublesome questions can be mostly confined to the committees, which will contain the representative members of all parties. [See Reports of Committees, § 29.]

23. **To Amend.** This motion takes precedence of nothing but the question which it proposed to amend, and yields to any Privileged [§ 9], Incidental [§ 8] or Subsidiary [§ 7] Question, except to Indefinitely Postpone. It can be amended itself, but this "amendment of an amendment" cannot be amended. An Amendment may be inconsistent with one already adopted, or may directly conflict with the spirit of the original motion, but it must have a direct bearing upon the subject of that motion. *To illustrate*: a motion for a vote of thanks could be amended by substituting for

"thanks" the word "censure;" or one condemning certain customs could be amended by adding other customs.

An Amendment may be in any of the following forms: (a) to "add or insert" certain words or paragraphs; (b) to "strike out" certain words or paragraphs, the question, however, being stated by the Chair thus: "Shall these words (or paragraphs) stand as a part of the resolution?" and if this is adopted (that is, the motion to "strike out," fails) it does not preclude either amendment or a motion to "strike out and insert;" (c) "to strike certain words and insert others," which motion is indivisible, and if lost does not preclude another motion to strike out the same words and insert different ones; (d) to "substitute" another motion on the same subject for the one pending; (e) to "divide the question" into two or more questions, as the mover specifies, so as to get a separate vote on any particular point or points [see § 4].

If a paragraph is inserted it should be perfected by its friends previous to voting on it, as when once inserted it cannot be struck out or amended except by adding to it. The same is true in regard to words to be inserted in a resolution, as when once inserted they cannot be struck out, except by a motion to strike out the paragraph, or such a portion of it as shall make the question an entirely different one from that of inserting the particular words. The principle involved is that when the assembly has voted that certain words shall form a part of a resolution, it is not in order to make another motion which involves exactly the same question as the one they have decided. The only way to bring it up again is to move a Reconsideration [§ 27] of the vote by which the words were inserted.

In stating the question on an Amendment the Chairman should read (1) the passage to be amended; (2) the words to be struck out, if any; (3) the words to be inserted, if any; and (4) the whole passage as it will stand if the amendment is adopted. [For amending reports of committees, and propositions containing several paragraphs, see § 44.]

The numbers prefixed to paragraphs are only marginal indications, and should be corrected, if necessary, by the clerk, without any motion to amend.

The following motions cannot be amended:

To Adjourn (when unqualified) .... § 11.
For the Orders of the Day .... § 12.
All Incidental Questions .... § 8.
To Lie on the Table .... § 19.
For the Previous Question .... § 20.
An Amendment of an Amendment .... § 23.
To Postpone Indefinitely .... § 24.
Reconsider .... § 27.

An Amendment to Rules of Order, By-Laws or a Constitution shall require previous notice and a two-thirds vote for its adoption [see § 45].

24. **To Postpone Indefinitely.** This motion takes precedence of nothing except the Principal Question [§ 6], and yields to any Privileged [§ 9], Incidental [§ 8] or Subsidiary [§ 7] Motion, except to Amend. It cannot be amended; it opens to debate the entire question which it is proposed to postpone. Its effect is to entirely remove the question from before the assembly for that session [§ 42].

The Previous Question [§ 20], if ordered when this motion is pending, applies only to it without affecting the main question.

Miscellaneous Motions.

[§§ 25–27.]

25. **Filling Blanks.** In filling blanks the largest sum and the longest time proposed shall be first put to the question. Sometimes the most convenient way of amending a resolution is to create a blank by moving to strike out a certain number or time. It is customary for any number of members to propose numbers to fill a blank without the formality of a motion, these different propositions not being regarded in the light of amendments.

Nominations are treated in a similar manner, so that the second nomination, instead of being an amendment to the first, is an independent motion, which, if the first fails, is to be immediately voted upon. Any number of nominations can be made, the Chairman announcing each name as he hears it, and they should be voted upon in the order announced, until one receives a vote sufficient for an election.

26. **Renewal of a Motion.** When any Principal Question [§ 6] or Amendment has been once acted upon by the assembly, it cannot be taken up again at the same session [§ 42] except by a motion to Reconsider [§ 27]. The motion to Adjourn can be renewed if there has been progress in debate, or any business transacted. As a general rule the introduction of any motion that alters the state of affairs makes it admissible to renew any Privileged or Incidental motion (excepting Suspension of the Rules as provided in § 18), or Subsidiary motion (excepting an amendment), as in such a case the real question before the assembly is a different one.

To illustrate: a motion that a question lie on the table having failed, suppose afterwards it be moved to refer the matter to a committee, it is now in order to move again that the subject lie on the table; but such a motion would not be in order, if it were not made till after the failure of the motion to commit, as the question then resumes its previous condition.

When a subject has been referred to a committee which reports at the same meeting, the matter stands before the assembly as if it had been introduced for the first time. A motion which has been withdrawn has not been acted upon, and therefore can be renewed.

27. **Reconsider.** It is in order at any time, even when another member has the floor, or while the assembly is voting on the motion to Adjourn, during the day* on which a motion has been acted upon, to move to "Reconsider the vote" and have such motion "entered on the record," but it cannot be considered while another question is before the assembly. It must be made, excepting when the vote is by ballot, by a member who voted with the

---

* In Congress any one can move a reconsideration, excepting where the vote is taken by yeas and nays [§ 38], when the rule above applies. The motion can be made on the same or succeeding day.

prevailing side; for instance, in case a motion fails to pass for lack of a two-thirds vote, a reconsideration must be moved by one who voted against the motion.

A motion to reconsider the vote on a Subsidiary [§ 7] motion takes precedence of the main question. It yields to Privileged [§ 9] questions (except for the Orders of the Day), and Incidental [§ 8] questions.

This motion can be *applied** to every question, except to Adjourn and to Suspend the Rules. It is debatable or not, just as the question to be reconsidered is debatable or undebatable [§ 35]; when debatable, it opens up for discussion the entire subject to be reconsidered, and can have the Previous question [§ 20] applied to it without affecting anything but the motion to reconsider. It can be laid on the table [§ 19], and in such cases the last motion cannot be reconsidered; it is quite common and allowable to combine these two motions (though they must be voted on separately); in this case, the reconsideration like any other question, can be taken from the table, but possesses no privilege.† The motion to reconsider being laid on the table does not carry with it the pending measure. If an amendment to a motion has been either adopted or rejected, and then a vote taken on the motion as amended, it is not in order to reconsider the vote on the amendment until after the vote on the original motion has been reconsidered. If anything which the assembly cannot reverse, has been done as the result a vote, then that vote cannot be reconsidered.

The *Effect of making* this motion is to suspend all action that the original motion would have required until the reconsideration is acted upon; but if it is not called up, its effect terminates with the

---

* It is not the practice to reconsider an affirmative vote on the motion to lie on the table, as the same result can be more easily reached by the motion to take from the table. For a similar reason, an affirmative vote on the motion to take from the table cannot be reconsidered.

† In Congress this is a common method used by the friends of a measure to prevent its reconsideration.

session [§ 42], provided,* that in an assembly having regular meetings as often as monthly, if no adjourned meeting upon another day is held of the one at which the reconsideration was moved, its effect shall not terminate till the close of the next succeeding session. [See note at end of this section.] While this motion is so highly privileged as far as relates to having it entered on the minutes, yet the reconsideration of another question cannot be made to interfere with the discussion of a question before the assembly, but as soon as that subject is disposed of, the reconsideration, if called up, takes precedence of every thing except the motions to adjourn, and to fix the time to which to adjourn. As long as its effect lasts (as shown above), any one can call up the motion to reconsider and have it acted upon—excepting that when its effect extends beyond the meeting at which the motion was made, no one but the mover can call it up at that meeting. But the reconsideration of an Incidental [§ 8] or Subsidiary [§ 7] motion shall be immediately acted upon, as otherwise it would prevent action on the main question.

The *Effect of the adoption* of this motion is to place before the assembly the original question in the exact position it occupied before it was voted upon; consequently no one can debate the question reconsidered who had previously exhausted his right of debate [§ 34] on that question; his only resource is to discuss the question while the motion to reconsider is before the assembly.

When a vote taken under the operation of the previous question [§ 20] is reconsidered, the question is then divested of the previous question, and is open to debate and amendment, provided the previous question had been exhausted [see latter part of § 20] by votes taken on all the questions covered by it, before the motion to reconsider was made.

A reconsideration requires only a majority vote, regardless of the vote necessary to adopt the motion reconsidered. [For reconsidering in committee see § 28.]

---

* In Congress the effect always terminates with the session, and it cannot be called up by any one but the mover, until the expiration of the time during which it is in order to move a reconsideration.

Note On Reconsider.—In the English Parliament a vote once taken cannot be reconsidered, but in our Congress it is allowed to move a reconsideration of the vote on the same or succeeding day, and after the close of the last day for making the motion, any one can call up the motion to reconsider, so that this motion cannot delay action more than two days, and the effect of the motion, if not acted upon, terminates with the session. There seems to be no reason or good precedent for permitting merely two persons, by moving a reconsideration, to suspend for any length of time all action under resolutions adopted by the assembly, and yet where the delay is very short the advantages of reconsideration overbalance the evils.

Where a permanent society has meetings weekly or monthly, and usually only a small proportion of the society is present, it seems best to allow a reconsideration to hold over to another meeting, so that the society may have notice of what action is about to be taken. To prevent the motion being used to defeat a measure that cannot be deferred till the next regular meeting, it is provided that in case the society adjourn, to meet the next day for instance, then the reconsideration will not hold over beyond that session; this allows sufficient delay to notify the society, while, if the question is one requiring immediate action, the delay cannot extend beyond the day to which they adjourn. Where the meetings are only quarterly or annual, the society should be properly represented at each meeting, and their best interests are subserved by following the practice of Congress, and letting the effect of the reconsideration terminate with the session.

Art. IV. Committees and Informal Action.

[§§ 28–33.]

28. **Committees.** It is usual in deliberative assemblies, to have all preliminary work in the preparation of matter for their action, done by means of committees. These may be either "standing

committees" (which are appointed for the session [§ 42], or for some definite time, as one year); or "select committees," appointed for a special purpose; or a "committee of the whole" [§ 32], consisting of the entire assembly. [For method of appointing committees of the whole, see § 32; other committees, see commit, § 22.] The first person named on a committee is chairman, and should act as such, without the committee should see fit to elect another chairman, which they are competent to do. The clerk should furnish him, or some other member of the committee, with notice of the appointment of the committee, giving the names of the members, the matter referred to them, and such instructions as the assembly have decided upon. The chairman shall call the committee together, and if there is a quorum (a majority of the committee, see § 43), he should read or have read, the entire resolutions referred to them; he should then read each paragraph, and pause for amendments to be offered; when the amendments to that paragraph are voted on he proceeds to the next, only taking votes on amendments, as the committee cannot vote on the adoption of matter referred to them by the assembly.

If the committee originate the resolutions, they vote, in the same way, on amendments to each paragraph of the draft of the resolutions, (which draft has been previously prepared by one of their members or a sub-committee); they do not vote on the separate paragraphs, but having completed the amendments, they vote on the adoption of the entire report. When there is a preamble, it is considered last. If the report originates with the committee, all amendments are to be incorporated in the report; but, if the resolutions were referred, the committee cannot alter the text, but must submit the original paper intact, with their amendments (which may be in the form of a substitute, § 23) written on a separate sheet.

A committee is a miniature assembly that must meet together in order to transact business, and usually one of its members should be appointed its clerk. Whatever is not agreed to by the majority of the members present at a meeting (at which a quorum, consisting of a majority of the members of the committee, shall be present) cannot form a part of its report. The minority may be permitted to submit their views in writing also, either together, or each member separately, but their reports can only be acted upon, by voting to substitute one of them for the report of the committee. The rules of the assembly, as far as possible, shall apply in committee; but a reconsideration [§ 27] of a vote shall be allowed, regardless of the time elapsed, only when every member who voted with the majority is present when the reconsideration is moved.* A committee (except a committee of the whole, § 32) may appoint a sub-committee. When through with the business assigned them, a motion is made for the committee to "rise" (which is equivalent to the motion to adjourn), and that the chairman (or some member who is more familiar with the subject) make its report to the assembly. The committee ceases to exist as soon as the assembly receives the report [§ 30].

The committee has no power to punish its members for disorderly conduct, its resource being to report the facts to the assembly. No allusion can be made in the assembly to what has occurred in committee, except it be by a report of the committee, or by general consent. It is the duty of a committee to meet on the call of any two its of members, if the chairman be absent or decline to appoint such meeting. When a committee adjourns without appointing a time for the next meeting, it is called together in the same way as at its first meeting. When a committee adjourns to meet at another time, it is not necessary (though usually advisable) that absent members should be notified of the adjourned meeting.

---

* Both the English common parliamentary law and the rules of Congress prohibit the reconsideration of a vote by a committee; but the strict enforcement of this rule in ordinary committees, would interfere with rather than assist the transaction of business. The rule given above seems more just, and more in accordance with the practice of ordinary committees, who usually reconsider at pleasure. No improper advantage can be taken of the privilege, as long as every member who voted with the majority must be present when the reconsideration is moved.

29. **Forms of Reports of Committees.** The form of a report is usually similar to the following:

A standing committee reports thus: "The committee on [insert name of committee] respectfully report," [or "beg leave to report," or "beg leave to submit the following report,"] etc., letting the report follow.

A select or special committee reports as follows: "The committee to which was referred [state the matter referred] having considered the same respectfully report," etc. Or for "The committee" is sometimes written "Your committee," or "The undersigned, a committee."

When a minority report is submitted, it should be in this form (the majority reporting as above): "The undersigned, a minority of a committee to which was referred," etc. The majority report is the report of the committee, and should never be made out as the report of the majority.

All reports conclude with, "All of which is respectfully submitted." They are sometimes signed only by the chairman of the committee, but if the matter is of much importance, it is better that the report be signed by every member who concurs. The report is not usually dated, or addressed, but can be headed, as for example, "Report of the Finance Committee of the Y. P. A., on Renting a Hall."

30. **Reception of Reports.** When the report of a committee is to be made, the chairman (or member appointed to make the report) informs the assembly that the committee to whom was referred such a subject or paper, has directed him to make a report thereon, or report it with or without amendment, as the case may be; either he or any other member may move that it be "received"* now or at some other specified time.

---

* A very common error is, after a report has been read, to move that it be received; whereas, the fact that it has been read, shows that it has been already received by the assembly. Another mistake, less common, but dangerous, is to vote that the report be accepted (which is equivalent to adopting it, see § 31), when the intention is only to have the report up for consideration and afterwards move its adoption. Still a third error is to move that "the report be adopted and the committee discharged," when

Usually the formality of a vote on the reception of a report of a committee is dispensed with, the time being settled by general consent. Should any one object, a formal motion becomes necessary. When the time arrives for the assembly to receive the report, the chairman of the committee reads it in his place, and then delivers it to the clerk, when it lies on the table till the assembly sees fit to consider it. If the report consists of a paper with amendments, the chairman of the committee reads the amendments with the coherence in the paper, explaining the alterations and reasons of the committee for the amendments, till he has gone through the whole. If the report is very long, it is not usually read until the assembly is ready to consider it [see §§ 31, 44].

When the report has been received, whether it has been read or not, the committee is thereby dissolved, and can act no more without it is revived by a vote to recommit. If the report is recommitted, all the parts of the report that have not been agreed to by the assembly, are ignored by the committee as if the report had never been made.

31. **Adoption of Reports.** When the assembly is to consider a report, a motion should be made to "adopt," "accept," or "agree to" the report, all of which, when carried, have the same effect, namely, to make the doings of the committee become the acts of the assembly, the same as if done by the assembly without the intervention of a committee. If the report contains merely a statement of opinion or facts, the motion should be to "accept" the report; if it also concludes with resolutions or certain propositions, the motion should be to "agree to" the resolutions, or to "adopt" the propositions. After the above motion is made, the matter stands before the assembly exactly the same as if there had been no committee, and the subject had been introduced by the motion of the

---

the committee have reported in full and their report been received, so that the committee has already ceased to exist. If the committee however have made but a partial report, or report progress, then it is in order to move that the committee be discharged from the further consideration of the subject.

member who made the report. [See § 34 for his privileges in debate, and § 44 for the method of treating a report containing several propositions, when being considered by the assembly.]

32. **Committee of the Whole.** When an assembly has to consider a subject which it does not wish to refer to a committee, and yet where the subject matter is not well digested and put into proper form for its definite action, or, when for any other reason, it is desirable for the assembly to consider a subject with all the freedom of an ordinary committee, it is the practice to refer the matter to the "Committee of the Whole."* If it is desired to consider the question at once, the motion is made, "That the assembly do now resolve itself into a committee of the whole to take under consideration," etc., specifying the subject. This is really a motion to "commit." [See § 22 for its order of precedence, etc.] If adopted, the Chairman immediately calls another member to the chair, and takes his place as a member of the committee. The committee is under the rules of the assembly, excepting as stated hereafter in this section.

The only motions in order are to amend and adopt, and that the committee "rise and report," as it cannot adjourn; nor can it order the "yeas and nays" [§ 38]. The only way to close or limit debate in committee of the whole, is for the assembly to vote that the debate in committee shall cease at a certain time, or that after a certain time no debate shall be allowed excepting on new amendments, and then only one speech in favor of and one against it, of say, five minutes each; or in some other way regulate the time for debate.†

---

* In large assemblies, such as the U.S. House of Representatives, where a member can speak to any question but once, the committee of the whole seems almost a necessity, as it allows the freest discussion of a subject, while at any time it can rise and thus bring into force the strict rules of the assembly.

† In Congress no motion to limit debate in committee of the whole is in order till after the subject has been already considered in committee of the whole. As no subject would probably be considered more than once in committee of the whole, in an ordinary society, the enforcement of this rule would practically prevent such a

If no limit is prescribed, any member may speak as often as he can get the floor, and as long each time as allowed in debate in the assembly, provided no one wishes the floor who has not spoken on that particular question. Debate having been closed at a particular time by order of the assembly, it is not competent for the committee, even by unanimous consent, to extend the time. The committee cannot refer the subject to another committee. Like other committees [§ 28], it cannot alter the text of any resolution referred to it; but if the resolution originated in the committee, then all the amendments are incorporated in it.

When it is through with the consideration of the subject referred to it, or if it wishes to adjourn, or to have the assembly limit debate, a motion is made that "the committee rise and report," etc., specifying the result of its proceedings. This motion "to rise" is equivalent to the motion to adjourn, in the assembly, and is always in order (except when another member has the floor), and is undebatable. As soon as this motion is adopted, the presiding officer takes the chair, and the chairman of the committee, having resumed his place in the assembly, arises and informs him, that "the committee have gone through the business referred to them, and that he is ready to make the report, when the assembly is ready to receive it;" or he will make such other report as will suit the case.

The clerk does not record the proceedings of the committee on the minutes, but should keep a memorandum of the proceedings for the use of the committee. In large assemblies the clerk vacates his chair, which is occupied by the chairman of the committee, and the assistant clerk acts as clerk of the committee. Should the committee get disorderly, and the chairman be unable to preserve order, the presiding officer can take the chair, and declare the

---

society from putting any limit to debate in the committee. The rule as given above, allows the society, whenever resolving itself into committee of the whole, to impose upon the debate in the committee, such restrictions as are allowed in Congress after the subject has already been considered in committee of the whole.

committee dissolved. The quorum of the committee of the whole is the same as that of the assembly [§ 43]. If the committee finds itself without a quorum, it can only rise and report the fact to the assembly, which in such a case would have to adjourn.

33. **Informal Consideration of a Question** (or acting as if in committee of the whole).

It has become customary in many assemblies, instead of going into committee of the whole, to consider the question "informally," and afterwards to act "formally." In a small assembly there is no objection to this.* While acting informally upon any resolutions, the assembly can only amend and adopt them, and without further motion the Chairman announces that "the assembly acting informally [or as in committee of the whole] has had such a subject under consideration, and has made certain amendments, which he will report." The subject comes before the assembly then as if reported by a committee. While acting informally, the Chairman retains his seat, as it is not necessary to move that the committee rise, but at any time the adoption of such motions as to adjourn, the previous question, to commit, or any motion except to amend or adopt, puts an end to the informal consideration; as for example, the motion to commit is equivalent to the following motions when in committee of the whole: (1) That the committee rise; (2) that the committee of the whole be discharged from the further consideration of the subject, and (3) that it be referred to a committee.

While acting informally, every member can speak as many times as he pleases, and as long each time as permitted in the assembly [§ 34], and the informal action may be rejected or altered

---

* In the U.S. Senate all bills, joint resolutions and treaties, upon their second reading are considered "as if the Senate were in committee of the whole," which is equivalent to considering them informally. [U.S. Senate Rules 28 and 38.] In large assemblies it is better to follow the practice of the House of Representatives, and go into committee of the whole.

by the assembly. While the clerk should keep a memorandum of the informal proceedings, it should not be entered on the minutes, being only for temporary use. The Chairman's report to the assembly of the informal action, should be entered on the minutes, as it belongs to the assembly's proceedings.

ART. V. DEBATE AND DECORUM.

[§§ 34–37.]

3 4. **Debate**.* When a motion is made and seconded, it shall be stated by the Chairman before being debated [see § 3]. When any member is about to speak in debate, he shall rise and respectfully address himself to "Mr. Chairman." ["Mr. President" is used where that is the designated title of the presiding officer; "Brother Moderator" is more common in religious meetings.] The Chairman shall then announce his name [see § 2]. By parliamentary courtesy, the member upon whose motion a subject is brought before the assembly is first entitled to the floor, even though another member has risen first and addressed the Chair; [in case of a report of a committee, it is the member who presents the report]; and this member is also entitled to close the debate, but not until every member choosing to speak, has spoken. This right to make the last speech upon the question, is not taken away by the Previous Question [§ 20] being ordered, or in any other way. With this exception, no member shall speak more than twice to the same question (only once to a question of order, § 14), nor longer than ten minutes at one time, without leave of the assembly, and the question upon granting the leave shall be decided by a majority vote without debate.† If greater freedom is desired, the proper course is to refer

---

* In connection with this section read §§ 1–5.

† The limit in time should vary to suit circumstances, but the limit of two speeches of ten minutes each will usually answer in ordinary assemblies, and it can be increased, when desirable, by a majority vote as shown above, or diminished as shown

the subject to the committee of the whole [§ 32], or to consider it informally [§ 33]. [For limiting or closing the debate, see § 37.]

No member can speak the second time to a question, until every member choosing to speak has spoken. But an amendment, or any other motion being offered, makes the real question before the assembly a different one, and, in regard to the right to debate, is treated as a new question. Merely asking a question, or making a suggestion, is not considered as speaking.

35. **Undebatable Questions.** The following questions shall be decided without debate, all others being debatable [see note at end of this section]:

To *Fix the Time to which the Assembly shall Adjourn* (when a
    privileged question, § 10).
To *Adjourn* [§ 11], (or in committee, *to rise*, which is used
    instead of to adjourn).
For the *Orders of the Day* [§ 13], and questions relating to
    the *priority of business*.
An *Appeal* [§ 14] when made while the Previous Question
    is pending, or when simply relating to indecorum or
    transgressions of the rules of speaking, or to the
    priority of business.
Objection to the Consideration of a Question [§ 15].
Questions relating to *Reading of Papers* [§ 16], or
    Withdrawing a Motion [§ 17], or *Suspending the Rules*
    [§ 18], or *extending the limits of debate* [§ 34], or *limiting
    or closing debate*, or granting *leave to continue his
    speech* to one who has been guilty of indecorum in
    debate [§ 36].

---

in § 37. In the U.S. House of Representatives no member can speak more than once to the same question, nor longer than one hour. The fourth rule of the Senate is as follows: "No Senator shall speak more than twice in any one debate on the same day, without leave of the Senate, which question shall be decided without debate." If no rule is adopted, each member can speak but once to the same question.

To *Lie on the Table* or to *Take from the Table* [§ 19].
The *Previous Question* [§ 20].
To *Reconsider* [§ 26] a question which is itself undebatable.

The motion to *Postpone to a certain time* [§ 21] allows of but very limited debate, which must be confined to the propriety of the postponement; but to *Reconsider a debatable question* [§ 26], or to *Commit* [§ 22], or *Indefinitely Postpone* [§ 24], opens the main question [§ 6] to debate. To *Amend* [§ 23] opens the main question to debate only so far as it is necessarily involved in the amendment.

The distinction between debate and making suggestions or asking a question, should always be kept in view, and when the latter will assist the assembly in determining the question, is allowed to a limited extent, even though the question before the assembly is undebatable.

Note On Undebatable Questions.—The English common parliamentary law makes all motions debatable, without there is a rule adopted limiting debate [Cushing's Manual, § 330]; but every assembly is obliged to restrict debate upon certain motions. The restrictions to debate prescribed in this section conform to the practice of Congress, where, however, it is very common to allow of brief remarks upon the most undebatable questions, sometimes five or six members speaking; this of course is allowed only when no one objects.

By examining the above list, it will be found, that, while free debate is allowed upon every principal question [§ 6], it is permitted or prohibited upon other questions in accordance with the following principles:

(a) Highly privileged questions, as a rule, should not be debated, as in that case they could be used to prevent the assembly from coming to a vote on the main question; (for instance, if the motion to adjourn were debatable, it could be used [see § 11] in a way to greatly hinder business). *High privilege is, as a rule, incompatible with the right of debate on the privileged question.*

(b) A motion that has the effect to suppress a question before the assembly, so that it cannot again be taken up that session [§ 42], allows of free debate. And a subsidiary motion [§ 7, except commit, which see below,] is debatable to just the extent that it interferes with the right of the assembly to take up the original question at its pleasure.

Illustrations: To "Indefinitely Postpone" [§ 24] a question, places it out of the power of the assembly to again take it up during that session, and consequently this motion allows of free debate, even involving the whole merits of the original question.

To "Postpone to a certain time" prevents the assembly taking up the question till the specified time, and therefore allows of limited debate upon the propriety of the postponement.

To "Lie on the Table" leaves the question so that the assembly can at any time consider it, and therefore should not be, and is not debatable.

To "Commit" would not be very debatable, according to this rule, but it is an exception, because it is often important that the committee should know the views of the assembly on the question, and it therefore is not only debatable, but opens to debate the whole question which it is proposed to refer to the committee.

36. **Decorum in Debate** [see § 2]. In debate a member must confine himself to the question before the assembly, and avoid personalities. He cannot reflect upon any act of the assembly, unless he intends to conclude his remarks with a motion to rescind such action, or else while debating such motion. In referring to another member, he should, as much as possible, avoid using his name, rather referring to him as "the member who spoke last," or in some other way describing him. The officers of the assembly should always be referred to by their official titles. It is not allowable to arraign the motives of a member, but the nature or

consequences of a measure may be condemned in strong terms. It is not the man, but the measure, that is the subject of debate. If at any time the Chairman rises to state a point of order, or give information, or otherwise speak, within his privilege [see § 40], the member speaking must take his seat till the Chairman has been first heard. When called to order, the member must sit down until the question of order is decided. If his remarks are decided to be improper, he cannot proceed, if any one objects, without the leave of the assembly expressed by a vote, upon which question there shall be no debate.

Disorderly words should be taken down by the member who objects to them, or by the clerk, and then read to the member; if he denies them, the assembly shall decide by a vote whether they are his words or not. If a member cannot justify the words he used, and will not suitably apologize for using them, it is the duty of the assembly to act in the case, requiring both members to withdraw* till it has decided its course, it being a general rule that no member should he present in the assembly when any matter relating to himself is under debate. If any business has taken place since the member spoke, it is too late to take notice of any disorderly words he used.

37. **Closing Debate.** Debate upon a question is not closed by the Chairman rising to put the question, as, until both the affirmative and negative are put, a member can claim the floor, and re-open debate [see § 38]. Debate can be closed by the following motions, which are undebatable [§ 35], and, except to Lie on the Table, shall require a two-thirds† vote for their adoption [§ 39]:

(a) *An objection to the consideration of a question* [only allowable when the question is first introduced, § 15], which, if sustained, not only stops debate, but also

---

* If both are personally interested. [See p. 102.]

† In Congress, where each speaker can occupy the floor one hour, any of these motions to cut off debate can be adopted by a mere majority. In ordinary societies harmony is so essential, that a two-thirds vote should be required to force the assembly to a final vote without allowing free debate.

throws the subject out of the assembly for that session [§ 42]; which latter effect is the one for which it was designed.

(b) To *lie on the table* [§ 19], which, if adopted, carries the question to the table, from which it cannot be taken without a majority favors such action.

(c) The *previous question* [§ 20], which has the effect of requiring all the questions before the assembly [excepting as limited in § 20] to be put to vote at once without further debate. It may be applied merely to an amendment or to an amendment of an amendment.

(d) For the assembly to adopt an *order* (1) *limiting debate* upon a special subject, either as to the number or length of the speeches; or (2) *closing debate* upon the subject at a stated time, when all pending questions shall be put to vote without further debate. Either of these two measures may be applied only to a pending amendment, or an amendment thereto, and when this is voted upon, the original question is still open to debate and amendment.

Art. VI. Vote.

[§§ 38–39.]

38. **Voting.** Whenever from the nature of the question it permits of no modification or debate, the Chairman immediately puts it to vote; if the question is debatable, when the Chairman thinks the debate has been brought to a close, he should inquire if the assembly is ready for the question, and if no one rises he puts the question to vote. There are various forms for putting the question, in use in different parts of the country. The rule in Congress, in the House of Representatives, is as follows: "Questions shall be distinctly put in this form, to-wit: 'As many as are of the opinion that (as the question may be) say *Aye*;' and after the affirmative voice

is expressed, 'As many as are of the contrary opinion, say *No.*' "The following form is very common: "It has been moved and seconded that (here state the question). As many as are favor of the motion say *Aye*; those opposed, *No.*" Or, if the motion is for the adoption of a certain resolution, after it has been read the Chairman can say, "You have heard the resolution read; those in favor of its adoption will hold up the right hand; those opposed will manifest it by the same sign." These examples are sufficient to show the usual methods of putting a question, the affirmative being always put first.

When a vote is taken, the Chairman should always announce the result in the following form: "The motion is carried—the resolution is adopted," or, "The ayes have it—the resolution is adopted." If, when he announces a vote, any member rises and states that he doubts the vote, or calls for a "division," the Chairman shall say, "A division is called for; those in favor of the motion will rise." After counting these, and announcing the number, he shall say, "Those opposed will rise." He will count these, announce the number, and declare the result; that is, whether the motion is carried or lost. Instead of counting the vote himself, he can appoint tellers to make the count and report to him. When tellers are appointed, they should be selected from both sides of the question. A member has the right to change his vote (when not made by ballot) before the decision of the question has been finally and conclusively pronounced by the Chair, but not afterwards.

Until the negative is put, it is in order for any member, in the same manner as if the voting had not been commenced, to rise and speak, make motions for amendment or otherwise, and thus renew the debate; and this, whether the member was in the assembly room or not when the question was put and the vote partly taken. In such case the question is in the same condition as if it had never been put.

No one can vote on a question affecting himself, but if more than one name is included in the resolution (though a sense of delicacy would prevent this right being exercised, excepting when it would change the vote) all are entitled to vote; for if this were not so, a minority could control an assembly by including the names of a sufficient number in a motion, say for preferring charges against them, and suspend them, or even expel them from the assembly. When there is a tie vote the motion fails, without the Chairman gives his vote for the affirmative, which in such case he can do. Where his vote will make a tie, he can cast it and thus defeat the measure.

Another form of voting is by *ballot*. This method is only adopted when required by the constitution or by-laws of the assembly, or when the assembly has ordered the vote to be so taken. The Chairman, in such cases, appoints at least two tellers, who distribute slips of paper upon which each member, including the Chairman,* writes his vote; the votes are then collected, counted by the tellers, and the result reported to the Chairman, who announces it to the assembly. The Chairman announces the result of the vote, in case of an election to office, in a manner similar to the following: "The whole number of votes cast is—; the number necessary for an election is—; Mr. A. received—; Mr. B.—; Mr. C.—. Mr. B. having received the required number is elected—." Where there is only one candidate for an office, and the constitution requires the vote to be by ballot, it is common to authorize the clerk to cast the vote of the assembly for such and such a person; if any one objects however, it is necessary to ballot in the usual way. So when a motion is made to make a vote unanimous, it fails if any one objects. In counting the ballots all blanks are ignored.

The assembly can by a majority vote order that the vote on any question be taken by *Yeas and Nays*.† In this method of voting the

---

* Should the Chairman neglect to vote before the ballots are counted, he cannot then vote without the permission of the assembly.

† Taking a vote by yeas and nays, which has the effect to place on the record how each member votes, is peculiar to this country, and while it consumes a great deal of time, is rarely useful in ordinary societies. By the Constitution, one-fifth of the members present can, in either house of Congress, order a vote to be taken by yeas and nays, and to avoid some of the resulting inconveniences various rules and customs

Chairman states both sides of the question at once; the clerk calls the roll and each member as his name is called rises and answers yes or no, and the clerk notes his answer. Upon the completion of the roll call the clerk reads over the names of those who answered the affirmative, and afterwards those in the negative, that mistakes may be corrected; he then gives the number voting on each side to the Chairman, who announces the result. An entry must be made in the minutes of the names of all voting in the affirmative, and also of those in the negative.

The form of putting a question upon which the vote has been ordered to be taken by yeas and nays, is similar to the following: "As many as are in favor of the adoption of these resolutions will, when their names are called, answer *yes* [or *aye*]—those opposed will answer *no*." The Chairman will then direct the clerk to call the roll. The negative being put at the same time as the affirmative, it is too late, after the question is put, to renew the debate. After the commencement of the roll call, it is too late to ask to be excused from voting. The yeas and nays cannot be ordered in committee of the whole [§ 32].

39. **Motions Requiring More than a Majority Vote**.* The following motions shall require a two-thirds vote for their adoption, as the right of discussion, and the right to have the rules enforced, should not be abridged by a mere majority:

---

have been established, which are ignored in this Manual, as according to it the yeas and nays can only be ordered by a majority, which prevents its being made use of to hinder business. In representative bodies it is very useful, especially where the proceedings are published, as it enables the people to know how their representatives voted on important measures. In some small bodies a vote on a resolution must be taken by yeas and nays, upon the demand of a single member.

*Where no rule to the contrary is adopted, a majority vote of the assembly, when a quorum [§ 43] is present, is sufficient for the adoption of any motion, except for the suspension of a rule, which can only be done by general consent, or unanimously. Congress requires a two-thirds vote for only the motions to suspend and to amend the Rules, to take up business out of its proper order, and to make a special order [see note to § 37].

An Objection to the Consideration of a Question..............§ 15.

To Take up a Question out of its proper order ....§ 13.

To Suspend the Rules...§ 18.

The Previous Question...§ 20.

To Close or Limit Debate ....§ 37.

To Amend the Rules (requires previous notice also)...........§ 43.

To Make a special order ....§ 13.

ART. VII. THE OFFICERS AND THE MINUTES.

[§§ 40–41.]

40. **Chairman* or President**. The presiding officer, when no special title has been assigned him, is ordinarily called the Chairman (or in religious assemblies more usually the Moderator); frequently the constitution of the assembly prescribes for him a title, such as President.

His duties are generally as follows:

To open the session at the time at which the assembly is to meet, by taking the chair and calling the members to order; to announce the business before the assembly in the order in which it is to be acted upon [§ 44]; to state and to put to vote [§ 38] all questions which are regularly moved, or necessarily arise in the course of proceedings, and to announce the result of the vote;

To restrain the members, when engaged in debate, within the rules of order; to enforce on all occasions the observance of order and decorum [§ 36] among the members, deciding all questions of order (subject to an appeal to the assembly by any two members, § 14), and to inform the assembly when necessary, or when referred to for the purpose, on a point of order or practice;

To authenticate, by his signature, when necessary, all the acts, orders and proceedings of the assembly, and in general to represent and stand for the assembly, declaring its will, and in all things obeying its commands.

---

* In connection with this section read § 44, and also § 40, 41.

The chairman shall rise* to put a question to vote, but may state it sitting; he shall also rise from his seat (without calling any one to the chair), when speaking to a question of order, which he can do in preference to other members. In referring to himself he should always use his official title thus: "The Chair decides so and so," not "I decide, &c." When a member has the floor, the chairman cannot interrupt him as long as he does not transgress any of the rules of the assembly, excepting as provided in § 2.

He is entitled to vote when the vote is by ballot,† and in all other cases where the vote would change the result. Thus in a case where two-thirds vote is necessary, and his vote thrown with the minority would prevent the adoption of the question, he can cast his vote; so also he can vote with the minority when it will produce a tie vote and thus cause the motion to fail. Whenever a motion is made referring especially to the chairman, the maker of the motion should put it to vote.

The chairman can, if it is necessary to vacate the chair, appoint a chairman *pro tem.*,‡ but the first adjournment puts an end to the appointment, which the assembly can terminate before, if it pleases, by electing another chairman. But the regular chairman, knowing that he will be absent from a future meeting, cannot authorize another member to act in his place at such meeting; the clerk [§ 41], or in his absence any member, should in such case call the meeting to order, and a chairman *pro tem.* be elected, who would hold office during that session [§ 42], without such office was terminated by the entrance of the regular chairman.

The chairman sometimes calls a member to the chair, and himself takes part in the debate. But this should rarely be done, and

---

* It is not customary for the chairman to rise while putting questions in very small bodies, such as committees, boards of trustees, &c.

† But this right is lost if he does not use it before the tellers have commenced to count the ballots. The assembly can give leave to the chairman to vote under such circumstances.

‡ When there are Vice Presidents, then the first one on the list that is present, is, by virtue of his office, chairman during the absence of the President, and should always be called to the chair when the President temporarily vacates it.

nothing can justify it in a case where much feeling is shown, and there is a liability to difficulty in preserving order. If the chairman has even the appearance of being a partisan, he loses much of his ability to control those who are on the opposite side of the question.* The chairman should not only be familiar with parliamentary usage, and set the example of strict conformity to it, but he should be a man of executive ability, capable of controlling men; and it should never be forgotten, that, to control others, it is necessary to control one's self. An excited chairman can scarcely fail to cause trouble in a meeting.

A chairman will often find himself perplexed with the difficulties attending his position, and in such cases he will do well to heed the advice of a distinguished writer on parliamentary law, and recollect that—"The great purpose of all rules and forms, is to subserve the will of the assembly, rather than to restrain it; to facilitate, and not to obstruct, the expression of their deliberate sense."

41. **Clerk or Secretary** [*and the Minutes*]. The recording officer is usually called the "Clerk" or "Secretary,"† and the record of

---

* The unfortunate habit many chairmen have of constantly speaking upon questions before the assembly, even interrupting the member who has the floor, is unjustified by either the common parliamentary law, or the practice of Congress. One who expects to take an active part in debate should never accept the chair. "It is a general rule, in all deliberative assemblies, that the presiding officer shall not participate in the debate, or other proceedings, in any other capacity than as such officer. He is only allowed, therefore, to state matters of fact within his knowledge; to inform the assembly on points of order or the course of proceeding, when called upon for that purpose, or when he finds it necessary to do so; and on appeals from his decision on questions of order, to address the assembly in debate." [Cushing's Manual, page 106.] "Though the Speaker [chairman] may of right speak to matters of order and be first heard, he is restrained from speaking on any other subject except where the assembly have occasion for facts within his knowledge; then he may, with their leave, state the matter of fact." [Jefferson's Manual, sec. xvii, and Barclay's "Digest of the Rules and Practice of the House of Representatives, U.S.," page 195.]

† When there are two secretaries, he is termed the "recording secretary," and the other one, the "corresponding secretary." In many societies the secretary, besides acting as recording officer, collects the dues of members, and thus becomes to a certain extent a financial officer. In most cases the treasurer acts as banker, only paying on the order of the society, signed by the secretary alone, or by the president and

proceedings the "Minutes." His desk should be near that of the chairman, and in the absence of the chairman, (if there is no vice president present) when the hour for opening the session arrives, it is his duty to call the meeting to order, and to preside until the election of a chairman *pro tem.*, which should be done immediately. He should keep a record of the proceedings, commencing in a form similar to the following:*

"At a regular quarterly meeting of [state the name of the society] held on the 31st day of March, 1875, at [state the place of meeting], the President in the chair, the minutes were read by the clerk and approved." If the regular clerk is absent, insert after the words "in the chair," the following: "The clerk being absent, Robert Smith was appointed clerk *pro tem.* The minutes were then read and approved." If the minutes were not read, say "the reading of the minutes was dispensed with." The above form will show the essentials, which are as follows: (a) The kind of meeting, "regular" [or stated] or "special," or "adjourned regular," or "adjourned special;" (6) name of the assembly; (c) date and place of meeting (excepting when the place is always the same); (d) the fact of the presence of the regular chairman and clerk, or in their absence the names of their substitutes; (e) whether the minutes of the previous meeting were approved.

The minutes should be signed by the person who acted as clerk for that meeting: in some societies the chairman must also sign them. When published, they should be signed by both officers.

In keeping the minutes much depends upon the kind of meeting, and whether the minutes are to be published. If they are to be published, it is often of far more interest to know what was

---

secretary. In such cases the secretary becomes in reality the financial officer of the society, and should make reports to the society, of funds received and from what sources, and of the funds expended and for what purposes. See § 52 for his duties as financial officer.

* See Clerk and Minutes in Part II, § 51.

said by the leading speakers, than to know what routine business was done, and what resolutions adopted. In such case the duties of the secretary are arduous, and he should have at least one assistant.

In ordinary society meetings and meetings of Boards of Managers and Trustees, on the contrary, there is no object in reporting the debates; the duty of the clerk, in such cases, is mainly to record what is "done" by the assembly, not what is said by the members. Without there is a rule to the contrary, he should enter every Principal motion [§ 6] that is before the assembly, whether it is adopted or rejected; and where there is a division [see Voting, § 38], or where the vote is by ballot, he should enter the number of votes on each side; and when the voting is by yeas and nays [§ 38], he should enter a list of the names of those voting on each side. He should endorse on the reports of committees, the date of their reception, and what further action was taken upon them, and preserve them among the records, for which he is responsible. He should in the minutes make a brief summary of a report that has been agreed to, except where it contains resolutions, in which case the resolutions will be entered in full as adopted by the assembly, and not as if it was the report accepted. The proceedings of the committee of the whole [§ 32], or while acting informally [§ 33], should not be entered on the minutes. Before an adjournment without day, it is customary to read over the minutes for approval, if the next meeting of the board or society will not occur for a long period. Where the regular meetings are not separated by too great a time, the minutes are read at the next meeting.

The clerk should, previous to each meeting, for the use of the chairman, make out an order of business [§ 44], showing in their exact order what is necessarily to come before the assembly. He should also have at each meeting a list of all standing committees, and such select committees as are in existence at the time. When a committee is appointed, he should hand the names of the committee and all papers referred to it to the chairman, or some other of its members.

ART. VIII. MISCELLANEOUS.

[§§ 42–45.]

42. **A Session** of an assembly is a meeting* which, though it may last for days, is virtually *one meeting*, as a session of a Convention; or even months, as a session of Congress; it terminates by an "adjournment without day." The intermediate adjournments from day to day, or the recesses taken during the day, do not destroy the continuity of the meeting—they in reality constitute one session. In the case of a permanent society, having regular meetings every week, month, or year, for example, each meeting constitutes a separate session of the society, which session however can be prolonged by adjourning to another day.

If a principal motion [§ 6] is indefinitely postponed or rejected at one session, while it cannot be introduced again at the same session [see Renewal of a Motion, § 26], it can be at the next, without it is prohibited by a rule of the assembly.

No one session of the assembly can interfere with the rights of the assembly at any future session,† without it is expressly so provided in their Constitution, Bylaws, or Rules of Order, all of which are so guarded (by requiring notice of amendments, and at least a two-thirds vote for their adoption) that they are not subject to sudden changes, but may be considered as expressing the deliberate views of the whole society, rather than the opinions or wishes of any particular meeting. Thus, if the presiding officer were ill, it would not be competent for one session of the assembly to elect a chairman to hold office longer than that session, as it cannot control or dictate to the next session of the assembly. By going

---

* See definitions in Introduction for the distinction between "meeting" and "session."

† Any one session can adopt a rule or resolution of a permanent nature, and it continues in force until at some future session it is rescinded. But these Standing Rules, as they are termed, do not interfere with future sessions, because at any moment a majority can suspend or rescind them, or adopt new ones.

through the prescribed routine of an election to fill the vacancy, giving whatever notice is required, it could then legally elect a chairman to hold office while the vacancy lasted. So it is improper for an assembly to postpone anything to a day beyond the next succeeding session, and thus attempt to prevent the next session from considering the question. On the other hand, it is not permitted to move a reconsideration [§ 27] of a vote taken at a previous session [though the motion to reconsider can be called up, provided it was made at the last meeting of the previous session]. Committees can be appointed to report at a future session.

Note On Session—In Congress, and in fact all legislative bodies, the limits of the sessions are clearly defined; but in ordinary societies having a permanent existence, with regular meetings more or less frequent, there appears to be a great deal of confusion upon the subject. Any society is competent to decide what shall constitute one of its sessions, but, where there is no rule on the subject, the common parliamentary law would make each of its regular or special meetings a separate session, as they are regarded in this Manual.

The disadvantages of a rule making a session include all the meetings of an ordinary society, held during a long time as one year, are very great. [Examine Indefinitely Postpone, § 24, and Renewal of a Motion, § 26.] If members of any society take advantage of the freedom allowed by considering each regular meeting a separate session, and repeatedly renew obnoxious or unprofitable motions, the society can adopt a rule prohibiting the second introduction of any principal question [§ 6] within, say, three or six months after its rejection, or indefinite postponement, or after the society has refused to consider it. But generally it is better to suppress the motion by refusing to consider it [§ 15].

43. **A Quorum** of an assembly is such a number as is competent to transact its business. Without there is a special rule on the subject, the quorum of every assembly is a majority of all the members of the assembly. But whenever a society has any permanent existence, it is usual to adopt a much smaller number, the

quorum being often less than one-twentieth of its members; this becomes a necessity in most large societies, where only a small fraction of the members are ever present at a meeting.*

The Chairman should not take the chair till a quorum is present, except where there is no hope of there being a quorum, and then no business can be transacted, except simply to adjourn. So whenever during the meeting there is found not to be a quorum present, the only thing to be done is to adjourn—though if no question is raised about it, the debate can be continued, but no vote taken, except to adjourn.

In committee of the whole the quorum is the same as in the assembly; in any other committee the majority is a quorum, without the assembly order otherwise, and it must wait for a quorum before proceeding to business. If the number afterwards should be reduced below a quorum, business is not interrupted, unless a member calls attention to the fact; but no question can be decided except when a quorum is present. Boards of Trustees, Managers, Directors, etc., are on the same footing as committees, in regard to a quorum. Their power is delegated to them as a body, and what number shall be present in order that they may act as a Board, is to be decided by the society that appoints the Board. If no quorum is specified, then a majority constitutes a quorum.

44. **Order of Business.** It is customary for every society having a permanent existence, to adopt an order of business for its meetings. When no rule has been adopted, the following is the order:

(1) Reading the Minutes of the previous meeting [and their approval].
(2) Reports of Standing Committees.
(3) Reports of Select Committees.
(4) Unfinished Business.
(5) New Business.

---

*While a quorum is competent to transact any business, it is usually not expedient to transact important business without there is a fair attendance at the meeting, or else previous notice of such action has been given.

Boards of Managers, Trustees, etc., come under the head of standing committees. Questions that have been postponed from a previous meeting, come under the head of unfinished business; and if a subject has been made a "special order" for the day, it shall take precedence of all business except reading the minutes. If it is desired to transact business out of its order, it is necessary to suspend the rules [§ 18], which can only be done by a two-thirds vote; but as each subject comes up, a majority can at once lay it on the table [§ 19], and thus reach any question which they desire to first dispose of.

*The order of business, in considering any report or proposition containing several paragraphs,** is as follows:

The whole paper should be read entirely through by the clerk; then the Chairman should read it by paragraphs, pausing at the end of each, and asking, "Are there any amendments proposed to this paragraph?" If none are offered, he says, "No amendments being offered to this paragraph, the next will be read;" he then reads the next, and proceeds thus to the last paragraph, when he states that the whole report or resolutions have been read, and are open to amendment. He finally puts the question on agreeing to or adopting the whole paper as amended. If there is a preamble it should be read after the last paragraph.

If the paper has been reported back by a committee with amendments, the clerk reads only the amendments, and the Chairman then reads the first and puts it to the question, and so on till all the amendments are adopted or rejected, admitting amendments to the committee's amendments, but no others. When through with the committee's amendments, the Chairman pauses for any other amendments to be proposed by the assembly;

---

* No vote should be taken on the adoption of the several paragraphs,—one vote being taken finally on the adoption of the whole paper. By not adopting separately the different paragraphs, it is in order, after they have all been amended, to go back and amend any of them still further. In committee a similar paper would be treated the same way [see § 30]. In § 48 (b) an illustration is given of the practical application of this section.

and when these are voted on, he puts the question on agreeing to or adopting the paper as amended. Where the resolutions have been just read by the member presenting them, the reading by the clerk is usually dispensed with without the formality of a vote. By "suspending the rules" [§ 18], or by general consent, a report can be at once adopted without following any of the above routine.

45. **Amendments of Rules of Order.** These rules can be amended at any regular meeting of the assembly, by a two-thirds vote of the members present, provided the amendment was submitted in writing at the previous regular meeting. And no amendment to Constitutions or By-Laws shall be permitted, without at least equal notice and a two-thirds vote.*

---

* Constitutions, By-Laws and Rules of Order should always prohibit their being amended by less than a two-thirds vote, and without previous notice of the amendment being given. If the By-Laws should contain rules that it may be desirable to occasionally suspend, then they should state how they can be suspended, just as is done in these Rules of Order, § 18. If there is no such rule it is impossible to suspend any rule, if a single member objects.

PART II.

Organization and Conduct of Business.*

ART. IX. ORGANIZATION AND MEETINGS.

[§§ 46–49.]

46. **An Occasional or Mass Meeting**. (a) *Organization*. When a meeting is held which is not one of an organized society, shortly after the time appointed for the meeting, some member of the assembly steps forward and says: "The meeting will please come to order; I move that Mr. A. act as chairman of this meeting." Some one else says, "I second the motion." The first member then puts the question to vote, by saying, "It has been moved and seconded that Mr. A. act as chairman of this meeting; those in favor of the motion will say aye," and when the affirmative vote is taken, he says, "those opposed will say no." If the majority vote in the affirmative, he says, "The motion is carried; Mr. A. will take the chair." If the motion is lost, he announces that fact, and calls for the nomination of some one else for chairman, and proceeds with the new nomination as in the first case.†

---

* The exact words used by the chairman or member, are in many cases in quotations. It is not to be inferred that these are the only forms permitted, but that these forms are proper and common. They are inserted for the benefit of those unaccustomed to parliamentary forms, and are sufficiently numerous for ordinary meetings.

† Sometimes a member nominates a chairman and no vote is taken, the assembly signifying their approval by acclamation. The member who calls the meeting to order, instead of making the motion himself, may act as temporary chairman, and say: "The meeting will please come to order: will some one nominate a chairman?"

When Mr. A. takes the chair, he says, "The first business in order is the election of a secretary." Some one then makes a motion as just described, or he says "I nominate Mr. B," when the chairman puts the question as before. Sometimes several names are called out, and the chairman, as he hears them, says, "Mr. B. is nominated; Mr. C. is nominated," etc; he then takes a vote on the first one he heard, putting the question thus: "As many as are in favor of Mr. B. acting as secretary of this meeting, will say aye; those opposed will say no." If the motion is lost the question is put on Mr. C., and so on, till some one is elected. In large meetings the secretary takes his seat near the chairman: he should in all cases keep a record of the proceedings, as described in § 51.

(b) *Adoption of Resolutions.* These two officers are all that are usually necessary for a meeting; so, when the secretary is elected, the chairman asks, "What is the further pleasure of the meeting?" If the meeting is merely a public assembly called together to consider some special subject, it is customary at this stage of the proceedings for some one to offer a series of resolutions previously prepared, or else to move the appointment of a committee to prepare resolutions upon the subject. In the first case he rises and says, "Mr. Chairman;" the chairman responds, "Mr. C." Mr. C., having thus obtained the floor, then says, "I move the adoption of the following resolutions," which he then reads and hands to the chairman;* some one else says, "I second the motion." The

---

He puts the question to vote on the nomination as described above. In large assemblies, the member who nominates, with one other member, frequently conducts the presiding officer to the chair, and the chairman makes a short speech, thanking the assembly for the honor conferred on him.

* The practice in legislative bodies, is to send to the clerk's desk all resolutions, bills, etc., the title of the bill and the name of the member introducing it, being endorsed on each. In such bodies, however, there are several clerks and only one chairman. In many assemblies there is but one clerk or secretary, and, as he has to keep the minutes, there is no reason for his being constantly interrupted to read every resolution offered. In such assemblies, without there is a rule or established custom to the contrary, it is allowable, and frequently much better, to hand all resolutions,

chairman sometimes directs the secretary to read the resolutions again, after which he says, "The question is on the adoption of the resolutions just read," and if no one rises immediately, he adds, "Are you ready for the question?" If no one then rises, he says, "As many as are in favor of the adoption of the resolutions just read, will say aye;" after the ayes have voted, he says, "As many as are of a contrary opinion will say no;" he then announces the result of the vote as follows: "The motion is carried—the resolutions are adopted," or, "The ayes have it—the resolutions are adopted."

(c) *Committee to draft Resolutions.* If it is preferred to appoint a committee to draft resolutions, a member, after he has addressed the Chair and been recognized, says, "I move that a committee be appointed to draft resolutions expressive of the sense of this meeting on," etc., adding the subject for which the meeting was called. This motion being seconded, the Chairman states the question [§ 67] and asks, "Are you ready for the question?" If no one rises, he puts the question, announces the result, and, if it is carried, he asks, "Of how many shall the committee consist?" If only one number is suggested, he announces that the committee will consist of that number; if several numbers are suggested, he states the different ones and then takes a vote on each, beginning with the largest, until one number is selected.

He then inquires, "How shall the committee be appointed?" This is usually decided without the formality of a vote. The committee may be "appointed" by the Chair—in which case the chairman names the committee and no vote is taken; or the committee may be "nominated" by the Chair, or the members of the assembly (no member naming more than one, except by unanimous consent), and then the assembly vote on their appointment. When the chairman nominates, after stating the names he puts one

---

reports, etc., directly to the chairman. If they were read by the member introducing them, and no one calls for another reading, the chairman can omit reading them when he thinks they are fully understood. In reference to the manner of reading and stating the question, when the resolution contains several paragraphs, see § 44.

question on the entire committee, thus: "As many as are in favor of these gentlemen constituting the committee, will say aye." If nominations are made by members of the assembly, and more names mentioned than the number of the committee, a separate vote should be taken on each name. (In a mass meeting it is safer to have all committees appointed by the chairman.)

When the committee are appointed they should at once retire and agree upon a report, which should be written out as described in § 53. During their absence other business may be attended to, or the time may be occupied with hearing addresses. Upon their return the chairman of the committee (who is the one first named on the committee, and who quite commonly, though not necessarily, is the one who made the motion to appoint the committee), avails himself of the first opportunity to obtain the floor [see § 2], when he says, "The committee appointed to draft resolutions, are prepared to report." The chairman tells him that the assembly will now hear the report, which is then read by the chairman of the committee, and handed to the presiding officer, upon which the committee is dissolved without any action of the assembly.

A member then moves the "adoption" or "acceptance" of the report, or that "the resolutions be agreed to," which motions have the same effect if carried, namely, to make the resolutions the resolutions of the assembly just as if the committee had had nothing to do with them.* When one of these motions is made, the chairman acts as stated above when the resolutions were offered by a member. If it is not desired to immediately adopt the resolutions, they can be debated, modified, their consideration postponed, etc., as explained in §§ 55–63.

When through with the business for which the assembly were convened, or when from any other cause it is desirable to close the

---

* A very common error is, after a report has been read, to move that it be received; whereas, the fact that it has been read, shows that it has been already received by the assembly. Another mistake, less common but dangerous, is to vote that the report be accepted (which is equivalent to adopting it), when the intention is only to have the report up for consideration and afterwards move its adoption.

meeting, some one moves "to adjourn;" if the motion is carried and no other time for meeting has been appointed, the chairman says, "The motion is carried;—this assembly stands adjourned without day." [Another method by which the meeting may be conducted is shown in § 48.]

(d) *Additional Officers.* If more officers are required than a chairman and secretary, they can be appointed before introducing the resolutions, in the manner described for those officers; or the assembly can first form a temporary organization in the manner already described, only adding "pro tem." to the title of the officers, thus: "chairman pro tem." In this latter case, as soon as the secretary pro tem. is elected, a committee is appointed to nominate the permanent officers, as in the case of a convention [§ 47]. Frequently the presiding officer is called the President, and sometimes there is a large number of Vice Presidents appointed for mere complimentary purposes. The Vice Presidents in large formal meetings, sit on the platform beside the President, and in his absence, or when he vacates the chair, the first on the list that is present should take the chair.

47. **Meeting of a Convention or Assembly of Delegates.** If the members of the assembly have been elected or appointed as members, it becomes necessary to know who are properly members of the assembly and entitled to vote, before the permanent organization is effected. In this case a temporary organization is made, as already described, by the election of a chairman and secretary "pro tem.," when the chairman announces, "The next business in order is the appointment of a committee on credentials." A motion may then be made covering the entire case, thus: "I move that a committee of three on the credentials of members be appointed by the Chair, and that the committee report as soon as practicable;" or they may include only one of these details, thus: "I move that a committee be appointed on the credentials of members." In either case the Chair proceeds as already described in the cases of committees on resolutions [§ 46, (c)].

On the motion to accept the report of the committee, none can vote except those reported by the committee as having proper credentials. The committee, beside reporting a list of members with proper credentials, may report doubtful or contested cases, with recommendations, which the assembly may adopt, or reject, or postpone, etc. Only members whose right to their seats is undisputed, can vote.

The chairman, after the question of credentials is disposed of, at least for the time, announces that "The next business in order is the election of permanent officers of the assembly." Some one then moves the appointment of a committee to nominate the officers, in a form similar to this: "I move that a committee of three be appointed by the Chair to nominate the permanent officers of this convention." This motion is treated as already explained. When the committee make their report, some one moves "That the report of the committee be accepted and that the officers nominated be declared the officers of this convention."* This motion being carried, the chairman declares the officers elected, and instantly calls the new presiding officer to the chair, and the temporary secretary is at the same time replaced. The convention is now organized for work.

48. **A Permanent Society**. (a) *First Meeting*. When it is desired to form a permanent society, those interested in it should see that only the proper persons are invited to be present, at a certain time and place. It is not usual in mass meetings, or meetings called to organize a society, to commence until fifteen or thirty minutes after the appointed time, when some one steps forward and says, "The meeting will please come to order; I move that Mr. A. act as chairman of this meeting;" some one "seconds the motion," when

---

*Where there is any competition for the offices, it is better that they be elected by ballot. In this case, when the nominating committee report, a motion can be made as follows: "I move that the convention now proceed to ballot for its permanent officers;" or "I move that we now proceed to the election, by ballot, of the permanent officers of this convention." [See § 38, for balloting, and other methods of voting.] The constitutions of permanent societies usually provide that the officers shall be elected by ballot.

the one who made the motion puts it to vote (or, as it is called, "puts the question"), as already described, under an "occasional meeting" [§ 46, (a)]; and, as in that case, when the chairman is elected, he announces as the first business in order the election of a secretary.

After the secretary is elected, the chairman calls on some member who is most interested in getting up the society, to state the object of the meeting. When this member rises he says, "Mr. Chairman;" the chairman then announces his name, when the member proceeds to state the object of the meeting. Having finished his remarks, the chairman may call on other members to give their opinions upon the subject, and sometimes a particular speaker is called out by members who wish to hear him. The chairman should observe the wishes of the assembly, and while being careful not to be too strict, he must not permit any one to occupy too much time and weary the meeting.

When a sufficient time has been spent in this informal way, some one should offer a resolution, so that definite action can be taken. Those interested in getting up the meeting, if it is to be a large one, should have previously agreed upon what is to be done, and be prepared at the proper time to offer a suitable resolution, which may be in a form similar to this: "Resolved, That it is the sense of this meeting that a society for [state the object of the society] should now be formed in this city." This resolution, when seconded, and stated by the chairman, would be open to debate and be treated as already described [§ 46, (b)]. This preliminary motion could have been offered at the commencement of the meeting, and if the meeting is a very large one, this would probably be better than to have the informal discussion.

After this preliminary motion has been voted on, or even without waiting for such motion, one like this can be offered: "I move that a committee of five be appointed by the Chair, to draft a Constitution and By-Laws for a society for [here state the object], and that they report at an adjourned meeting of this assembly." This motion can be amended [§ 56] by striking out and adding words, etc., and it is debatable.

When this committee is appointed, the chairman may inquire, "Is there any other business to be attended to?" or, "What is the further pleasure of the meeting?" When all business is finished, a motion can be made to adjourn to meet at a certain place and time, which, when seconded, and stated by the Chair, is open to debate and amendment. It is usually better to fix the time of the next meeting [see § 63] at an earlier stage of the meeting, and then, when it is desired to close the meeting, move simply "to adjourn," which cannot be amended or debated. When this motion is carried, the chairman says, "This meeting stands adjourned to meet at," etc., specifying the time and place of the next meeting.

(b) *Second Meeting.** At the next meeting the officers of the previous meeting, if present, serve until the permanent officers are elected. When the hour arrives for the meeting, the chairman standing, says, "The meeting will please come to order:" as soon as the assembly is seated, he adds, "The secretary will read the minutes of the last meeting." If any one notices an error in the minutes, he can state the fact as soon as the secretary finishes reading them; if there is no objection, without waiting for a motion, the chairman directs the secretary to make the correction. The chairman then says, "If there is no objection the minutes will

---

* Ordinary meetings of a society are conducted like this second meeting, the chairman, however, announcing the business in the order prescribed by the rules of the society [§ 72]. For example, after the minutes are read and approved, he would say, "The next business in order is hearing reports from the standing committees." He may then call upon each committee in their order, for a report, thus: "Has the committee on applications for membership any report to make?" In which case the committee may report, as shown above, or some member of it reply that they have no report to make. Or, when the chairman knows that there are but few if any reports to make, it is better, after making the announcement of the business, for him to ask, "Have these committees any reports to make?" After a short pause, if no one rises to report, he states, "There being no reports from the standing committees, the next business in order is hearing the reports of select committees," when he will act the same as in the case of the standing committees. The chairman should always have a list of the committees, to enable him to call upon them, as well as to guide him in the appointment of new committees.

stand approved as read" [or "corrected," if any corrections have been made].

He announces as the next business in order, "the hearing of the report of the committee on the Constitution and By-Laws." The chairman of the committee, after addressing "Mr. Chairman" and being recognized, reads the committee's report and then hands it to the chairman.* If no motion is made, the chairman says, "You have heard the report read—what order shall be taken upon it?" Or simply inquires, "What shall be done with the report?" Some one moves its adoption, or still better, moves "the adoption of the Constitution reported by the committee," and when seconded, the chairman says, "The question is on the adoption of the Constitution reported by the committee." He then reads the first article of the Constitution, and asks, "Are there any amendments proposed to this article?" If none are offered, after a pause, he reads the next article and asks the same question, and proceeds thus until he reads the last article, when he says, "The whole Constitution having been read, it is open to amendment." Now any one can move amendments to any part of the Constitution.

When the chairman thinks it has been modified to suit the wishes of the assembly, he inquires, "Are you ready for the question?" If no one wishes to speak, he puts the question, "As many as are in favor of adopting the Constitution as amended, will say aye;" and then, "As many as are opposed, will say no." He distinctly announces the result of the vote, which should always be done. If the articles of the Constitution are subdivided into sections or paragraphs, then the amendments should be made by sections or paragraphs, instead of by articles.

The chairman now states that the Constitution having been adopted, it will be necessary for those wishing to become members

---

* In large and formal bodies the chairman, before inquiring what is to be done with the report, usually directs the secretary to read it again. See note to § 46 (c), for a few common errors in acting upon reports of committees. [See also note to § 46 (b).]

to sign it (and pay the initiation fee, if required by the Constitution), and suggests, if the assembly is a large one, that a recess be taken for the purpose. A motion is then made to take a recess for say ten minutes, or until the Constitution is signed. The constitution being signed, no one is permitted to vote excepting those who have signed it.

The recess having expired, the chairman calls the meeting to order and says, "The next business in order is the adoption of By-Laws." Some one moves the adoption of the By-Laws reported by the committee, and they are treated just like the Constitution. The chairman then asks, "What is the further pleasure of the meeting?" or states that the next business in order is the election of the permanent officers of the society. In either case some one moves the appointment of a committee to nominate the permanent officers of the society, which motion is treated as already described in § 47. As each officer is elected he replaces the temporary one, and when they are all elected the organization is completed.

If the society is one that expects to own real estate, it should be incorporated according to the laws of the state in which it is situated, and for this purpose, some one on the committee on the Constitution should consult a lawyer before this second meeting, so that the laws may be conformed to. In this case the trustees are usually instructed to take the proper measures to have the society incorporated.

49. **Constitutions, By-Laws, Rules of Order and Standing Rules**. In forming a Constitution and By-Laws, it is always best to procure copies of those adopted by several similar societies, and for the committee, after comparing them, to select one as the basis of their own, amending each article just as their own report is amended by the Society. When they have completed amending the Constitution, it is adopted by the committee. The By-Laws are treated in the same way, and then, having finished the work assigned them, some one moves, "That the committee rise, and that the chairman (or some other member) report the Constitution

and By-Laws to the assembly." If this is adopted, the Constitution and By-Laws are written out, and a brief report made of this form: "Your committee, appointed to draft a Constitution and By-Laws, would respectfully submit the following, with the recommendation that they be adopted as the Constitution and By-Laws of this society;" which is signed by all the members of the committee that concur in it. Sometimes the report is only signed by the chairman of the committee.

In the organization just given, it is assumed that both a Constitution and By-Laws are adopted. This is not always done; some societies adopt only a Constitution, and others only By-Laws. Where both are adopted, the constitution usually contains only the following:

(1) Name and object of the society.
(2) Qualification of members.
(3) Officers, their election and duties.
(4) Meetings of the society (only including what is essential, leaving details to the By-Laws).
(5) How to amend the Constitution.

These can be arranged in five articles, each article being subdivided into sections. The Constitution containing nothing but what is fundamental, it should be made very difficult to amend; usually previous notice of the amendment is required, and also a two-thirds or three-fourths vote for its adoption [§ 73]. It is better not to require a larger vote than two-thirds, and, where the meetings are frequent, an amendment should not be allowed to be made except at a quarterly or annual meeting, after having been proposed at the previous quarterly meeting.

The *By-Laws* contain all the other standing rules of the society, of such importance that they should be placed out of the power of any one meeting to modify; or they may omit the rules relating to the conduct of business in the meetings, which would then constitute the *Rules of Order* of the society. Every society, in its

By-Laws or Rules of Order, should adopt a rule like this: "The rules contained in—(specifying the work on parliamentary practice) shall govern the society in all cases to which they are applicable, and in which they are not inconsistent with the Rules of Order (or By-Laws) adopted by the society." Without such a rule, any one so disposed, could cause great trouble in a meeting.

In addition to the Constitution, By-Laws and Rules of Order, in nearly every society resolutions of a permanent nature are occasionally adopted, which are binding on the society until they are rescinded or modified. These are called *Standing Rules*, and can be adopted by a majority vote at any meeting. After they have been adopted, they cannot be modified at the same session except by a reconsideration [§ 60]. At any future session they can be suspended, modified or rescinded by a majority vote. The Standing Rules, then, comprise those rules of a society which have been adopted like ordinary resolutions, without the previous notice, etc., required for By-Laws, and consequently, future sessions of the society are at liberty to terminate them whenever they please. No Standing Rule (or other resolution) can be adopted which conflicts with the Constitution, By-Laws or Rules of Order.*

---

* In practice these various classes of rules are frequently very much mixed. The Standing Rules of some societies are really By-Laws, as the society cannot suspend them, nor can they be amended until previous notice is given. This produces confusion without any corresponding benefit.

Standing Rules should contain only such rules as are subject to the will of the majority of any meeting, and which it may be expedient to change at any time, without the delay incident to giving previous notice. Rules of Order should contain only the rules relating to the orderly transaction of the business in the meetings of the society. The By-Laws should contain all the other rules of the society which are of too great importance to be changed without giving notice to the society of such change; provided that the most important of these can be placed in a Constitution instead of in the By-Laws. These latter three should provide for their amendment. The Rules of Order should provide for their suspension. The By-Laws sometimes provide for the suspension of certain articles. None of these three can be suspended without it is expressly provided for.

ART. X. OFFICERS AND COMMITTEES.

[§§ 50–53.]

50. **Chairman or President.** It is the duty of the chairman to call the meeting to order at the appointed time, to preside at all the meetings, to announce the business before the assembly in its proper order, to state and put all questions properly brought before the assembly, to preserve order and decorum, and to decide all questions of order (subject to an appeal). When he "puts a question" to vote, and when speaking upon an appeal, he should stand;* in all other cases he can sit. In all cases where his vote would affect the result, or where the vote is by ballot, he can vote. When a member rises to speak, he should say, "Mr. Chairman," and the chairman should reply, "Mr. A;" he should not interrupt a speaker as long as he is in order, but should listen to his speech, which should be addressed to him and not to the assembly. The chairman should be careful to abstain from the appearance of partisanship, but he has the right to call another member to the chair while he addresses the assembly on a question; when speaking to a question of order he does not leave the chair.

51. **The Clerk, Secretary or Recording Secretary,** as he is variously called, should keep a record of the proceedings, the character of which depends upon the kind of meeting. In an occasional or mass meeting, the record usually amounts to nothing, but he should always record every resolution or motion that is adopted.

In a convention it is often desirable to keep a full record for publication, and where it lasts for several days, it is usual, and generally best, to appoint one or more assistant clerks. Frequently it is a tax on the judgment of the clerk to decide what to enter on the record, or the "Minutes," as it is usually called. Sometimes the points of each speech should be entered, and at other times

---

*In meetings of boards of managers, committees and other small bodies, the chairman usually retains his seat, and even members in speaking do not rise.

only the remark that the question was discussed by Messrs. A., B. and C. in the affirmative, and Messrs. D., E. and F. in the negative. Every resolution that is adopted should be entered, which can be done in this form: "On motion of Mr. D. it was resolved that, etc."

Sometimes a convention does its work by having certain topics previously assigned to certain speakers, who deliver formal addresses or essays, the subjects of which are afterwards open for discussion in short speeches, of five minutes, for instance. In such cases the minutes are very brief, without they are to be published, when they should contain either the entire addresses or carefully prepared abstracts of them, and should show the drift of the discussion that followed each one. In permanent societies, where the minutes are not published, they consist of a record of what was done and not what was said, and should be kept in a book.

The *Form* of the *Minutes* can be as follows:

> At a regular meeting of the M. L. Society, held in their hall, on Tuesday evening, March 16, 1875, Mr. A. in the chair and Mr. B. acting as secretary, the minutes of the previous meeting were read and approved. The committee on Applications reported the names of Messrs. C. and D. as applicants for membership; and on motion of Mr. F. they were admitted as members. The committee on—reported a series of resolutions, which were thoroughly discussed and amended, and finally adopted as follows:
>
> Resolved, That * * * * * * * * * * * * * * * *
> On motion of Mr. L. the society adjourned.
>
> L—B—,
> *Secretary.*

If the proceedings are to be published, the secretary should always examine the published proceedings of similar meetings, so as to conform to the custom, excepting where it is manifestly improper.

The Constitution, By-Laws, Rules of Order and Standing Rules should all be written in one book, leaving every other page blank; and whenever an amendment is made to any of them, it should be immediately entered on the page opposite to the article amended, with a reference to the date and page of the minutes where is recorded the action of the society.

The secretary has the custody of all papers belonging to the society, not specially under charge of any other officer. Sometimes his duties are also of a financial kind, when he should make such reports as are prescribed in the next section.

52. **Treasurer.** The duties of this officer vary in different societies. In probably the majority of cases he acts as a banker, merely holding the funds deposited with him, and paying them out on the order of the society signed by the secretary. His annual report, which is always required, in this case consists of merely a statement of the amount on hand at the commencement of the year, the amount received during the year (stating from what source received), the total amount paid out by order of the society, and the balance on hand. When this report is presented it is referred to an "auditing committee," consisting of one or two persons, who examine the treasurer's books and vouchers, and certify on his report that they "have examined his accounts and vouchers and find them correct, and the balance on hand is," etc., stating the amount on hand. The auditing committee's report being accepted is equivalent to a resolution of the society to the same effect, namely, that the treasurer's report is correct.

In the case here supposed, the real financial statement is made either by the board of trustees, or by the secretary or some other officer, according to the Constitution of the society. The principles involved, are, that every officer who receives money is to account for it in a report to the society, and that whatever officer is responsible for the disbursements, shall report them to the society. If the secretary, as in many societies, is really responsible for the expenses, the treasurer merely paying upon his order, then the secretary should make a full report of these expenses, so classified as to enable the society to readily see the amounts expended for various purposes.

It should always be remembered that the financial report is made for the information of members. The details of dates and separate payments for the same object, are a hinderance to its being understood, and are useless, as it is the duty of the auditing committee to examine into the details and see if the report is correct.

Every disbursing officer should be careful to get a receipt whenever he makes a payment; these receipts should be preserved in regular order, as they are the vouchers for the payments, which must be examined by the auditing committee. Disbursing officers cannot be too careful in keeping their accounts, and they should insist upon having their accounts audited every time they make a report, as by this means any error is quickly detected and may be corrected. When the society has accepted the auditing committee's report that the financial report is correct, the disbursing officer is relieved from the responsibility of the past, and if his vouchers were lost afterwards, it would cause no trouble. The best form for these financial reports depends upon the kind of society, and is best determined by examining those made in similar societies.

The following form can be varied to suit most cases: (when the statement of receipts and expenses is very long, it is often desirable to specify the amounts received from one or two particular sources, which can be done immediately after stating the total receipts; the same course can be taken in regard to the expenditures):

Treasurer's Report.

The undersigned, Treasurer of the M. L. Society, begs leave to submit the following annual report:

The balance on hand at the commencement of the year was ____ dollars and ____ cents. There was received from all sources during the year, ____ dollars and ____ cents; during the same time the expenses amounted to ____ dollars and ____ cents, leaving a balance on hand of ____ dollars and ____ cents.

The annexed statement of receipts and expenditures will show in detail the sources from which the receipts were obtained, and the objects to which the expenditures have been applied.

All of which is respectfully submitted.

S—M—,

Treasurer M. L. S.

The "Statement of receipts and expenditures" can be made, by simply giving a list of receipts, followed by a list of expenses, and finishing up with the balance on hand. The auditing committee's certificate to the correctness of the account should be written on the statement. Often the statement is made out in the form of an account, as follows:

Dr.   The M. L. S. in acct. with S. M., Treas.   *Cr.*

1874.		1874.	
Dec. 31. To rent of hall	$500 00	Jan. 1. By balance on hand from	
" Gas	80 00	last year's account	$21 13
" Stationery	26 50	Dec. 31. By initiation fees	95 00
" Janitor	360 00	" members' dues	875 00
" Balance on hand	24 63		
	$991 13		$991 13

We do hereby certify that we have examined the accounts and vouchers of the treasurer, and find them correct; and that the balance in his hands is twenty-four dollars and sixty-three cents.

R. V., J. L., *Audit Comm.*

53. **Committees.** In small assemblies, especially in those where but little business is done, there is not much need of committees. But in large assemblies, or in those doing a great deal of business, committees are of the utmost importance. When a committee is properly selected, in nine cases out of ten its action decides that of the assembly. A committee for *action* should be small and consist only of those heartily in favor of the proposed action. A committee

for deliberation or investigation, on the contrary, should be larger and represent all parties in the assembly, so that its opinion will carry with it as great weight as possible. The usefulness of the committee will be greatly impaired, if any important faction of the assembly be unrepresented on the committee. The appointment of a committee is fully explained in § 46 (c).

The first member named on a committee is their chairman, and it is his duty to call together the committee, and preside at their meetings. If he is absent, or from any cause fails or declines to call a meeting, it is the duty of the committee to assemble on the call of any two of their members. The committee are a miniature assembly, only being able to act when a quorum is present. If a paper is referred to them they must not deface it in any way, but write their amendments on a separate sheet. If they originate the paper, all amendments must be incorporated in it. When they originate the paper, usually one member has previously prepared a draft, which is read entirely through, and then read by paragraphs, the chairman pausing after each paragraph and asking, "Are there any amendments proposed to this paragraph?" No vote is taken on the adoption of the separate paragraphs, but after the whole paper has been read in this way, it is open to amendment, generally, by striking out any paragraph or inserting new ones, or by substituting an entirely new paper for it. When it has been amended to suit the committee, they should adopt it as their report, and direct the chairman or some other member to report it to the assembly. It is then written out, usually commencing in a style similar to this: "The committee to which was referred [state the matter referred], beg leave to submit the following report;" or, "Your committee appointed to [specify the object], would respectfully report," etc. It usually closes thus: "All of which is respectfully submitted," followed by the signatures of all the members concurring in the report, or sometimes by only that of the chairman.

If the minority submit a report, it commences thus: "The undersigned, a minority of the committee appointed," etc., continuing as the regular report of the committee. After the committee's report has been read, it is usual to allow the minority to present their report, but it cannot be acted upon except by a motion to substitute it for the report of the committee. When the committee's report is read, they are discharged without any motion. A motion to refer the paper back to the same committee (or to recommit), if adopted, revives the committee.

Art. XI. Introduction of Business.

[§ 54.]

54. Any member wishing to bring business before the assembly, should, without it is very simple, write down in the form of a motion, what he would like to have the assembly adopt, thus:

Resolved, That the thanks of this convention be tendered to the citizens of this community for their hearty welcome and generous hospitality.

When there is no other business before the assembly, he rises and addresses the chairman by his title, thus: "Mr. Chairman," who immediately recognizes him by announcing his name.* He, then having the floor, says that he "moves the adoption of the following resolution," which he reads and hands to the chairman.† Some one else seconds the motion, and the chairman says, "It has been moved and seconded that the following resolution be adopted," when he reads the resolution; or he may read the resolution and then state the question thus: "The question is on the adoption of the resolution just read." The merits of the resolution are then open to discussion, but before any member can discuss the question or make any motion, he must first obtain the floor as just described. After the chairman states the question, if no one rises

---

* If the chairman has any special title, as President, for instance, he should be addressed by it, thus: "Mr. President." Sometimes the chairman recognizes the speaker by merely bowing to him, but the proper course is to announce his name.

† Or, when he is recognized by the chair, he may say that he wishes to offer the following resolutions, which he reads and then moves their adoption.

to speak, or when he thinks the debate closed, he asks, "Are you ready for the question?" If no one then rises, he puts the question in a form similar to the following: "The question is on the adoption of the resolution which you have heard; as many as are in favor of its adoption will say aye." When the ayes have voted, he says, "As many as are of a contrary opinion will say no."* He then announces the result, stating that the motion is carried, or lost, as the case may be, in the following form: "The motion is carried—the resolution is adopted;" or, "The ayes have it—the resolution is adopted." A majority of the votes cast is sufficient for the adoption of any motion, excepting those mentioned in § 68.

ART. XII. MOTIONS.

[§§ 55–64.]

55. Motions Classified According to their Object. Instead of immediately adopting or rejecting a resolution as originally submitted, it may be desirable to dispose of it in some other way, and for this purpose various motions have come into use, which can be made while a resolution is being considered, and for the time being, supersede it. No one can make any of these motions while another member has the floor, excepting as shown in § 64, which see for the circumstances under which each motion can be made.

The following list comprises most of these motions, arranged in eight classes, according to the object for which each motion is used. [The names of the motions are printed in italics; each class is treated separately, as shown by the references.]

Motions Classified.
(1) To Amend or Modify..[§ 56]
    (a) *Amend.*
    (b) *Commit.*

---

* There are many other ways of putting a question; see § 67 and § 38. Other illustrations of the ordinary practice in introducing business will be seen in §§ 46–48.

(2) To Defer action .... [§ 57]
    (a) *Postpone to a certain time.*
    (b) *Lie on the Table.*
(3) To Suppress Debate.. [§ 58]
    (a) *Previous Question.*
    (b) *An Order limiting or closing Debate.*
(4) To Suppress the question .... [§ 59]
    (a) *Objection to its Consideration.*
    (b) *Postpone Indefinitely.*
    (c) *Lie on the Table.*
(5) To Consider a question the second time .... [§ 60]
    (a) *Reconsider.*
(6) Order and Rules... [§ 61]
    (a) *Orders of the day.*
    (b) *Special Orders.*
    (c) *Suspension of the Rules.*
    (d) *Questions of Order.*
    (e) *Appeal.*
(7) Miscellaneous... [§ 62]
    (a) *Reading of Papers.*
    (b) *Withdrawal of a Motion.*
    (c) *Questions of Privilege.*
(8) To close a meeting .... [§ 63]
    (a) *Fix the time to which to Adjourn.*
    (b) *Adjourn.*

56. **To Amend or Modify.** (a) *Amend.* If it is desired to modify the question in any way, the proper motion to make is to "amend," either by "adding" words, or by "striking out" words; or by "striking out certain words and inserting others;" or by "substituting" a different motion on the same subject for the one before the assembly; or by "dividing the question" into two or more questions, as the mover specifies, so as to get a separate vote on any particular point or points. Sometimes the enemies of a measure seek to amend it in such a way as to divide its friends, and thus defeat it.

When the amendment has been moved and seconded, the chairman should always state the question distinctly, so that every one may know exactly what is before them, reading first the paragraph which it is proposed to amend; then the words to be struck out, if there are any; next, the words to be inserted, if any; and finally, the paragraph as it will stand if the amendment is adopted. He then states that the question is on the adoption of the amendment, which is open to debate, the remarks being confined to the merits of the amendment, only going into the main question so far as is necessary in order to ascertain the propriety of adopting the amendment.

This amendment can be amended, but an "amendment of an amendment" cannot be amended. None of the undebatable motions mentioned in § 66, except to fix the time to which to adjourn, can be amended, nor can the motion to postpone indefinitely.

(b) *Commit.* If the original question is not well digested, or needs more amendment than can well be made in the assembly, it is usual to move "to refer it to a committee." This motion can be made while an amendment is pending, and it opens the whole merits of the question to debate. This motion can be amended by specifying the number of the committee, or how they shall be appointed, or when they shall report, or by giving them any other instructions. [See § 53 on committees, and § 46 (c) on their appointment.]

57. **To Defer Action**. (a) *Postpone to a certain time.* If it is desired to defer action upon a question till a particular time, the proper motion to make, is to "postpone it to that time." This motion allows of but limited debate, which must be confined to the propriety of the postponement to that time; it can be amended by altering the time, and this amendment allows of the same debate. The time specified must not be beyond that session [§ 70] of the assembly, except it be the next session, in which case it comes up with the unfinished business at the next session. This motion can be made when a motion to amend, or to commit or to postpone indefinitely, is pending.

(b) *Lie on the table.* Instead of postponing a question to a particular time, it may be desired to lay it aside temporarily until some other question is disposed of, retaining the privilege of resuming its consideration at any time.* The only way to accomplish this, is to move that the question "lie on the table." This motion allowing of neither debate nor amendment, the chairman immediately puts the question; if carried, the whole matter is laid aside until the assembly vote to "take it from the table" (which latter motion is undebatable and possesses no privilege). Sometimes this motion is used to suppress a measure, as shown in § 59 (c).

58. **To Suppress Debate.** (a) *Previous Question.* While as a general rule free debate is allowed upon every motion,† which, if adopted, has the effect of adopting the original question or removing it from before the assembly for the session,—yet, to prevent a minority from making an improper use of this privilege, it is necessary to have methods by which debate can be closed, and final action at once be taken upon a question.

To accomplish this, when any debatable question is before the assembly, it is only necessary for some one to obtain the floor and "call for the previous question;" this call being seconded, the chairman, as it allows of no debate, instantly puts the question, thus: "Shall the main question be now put?" If this is carried by a two-thirds vote [§ 68], all debate instantly ceases, excepting that the member who offered the original resolution, or reported it

---

* In Congress this motion is commonly used to defeat a measure, though it does not prevent a majority from taking it at any other time.] Some societies prohibit a question from being taken from the table, except by a two-thirds vote. This rule deprives the society of the advantages of the motion to "lie on the table." Because it would not be safe to lay a question aside temporarily, if one-third of the assembly were opposed to the measure, as that one-third could prevent its ever being taken from the table. A bare majority should not have the power, in ordinary societies, to adopt or reject a question, or prevent its consideration, without debate. See note at end of § 35 on the principles involved in making questions undebatable.

† Except an "objection to the consideration of the question" [§ 59 (a)]. See note to § 35 for a full discussion of this subject of debate.

from a committee, is, as in all other cases, entitled to the floor to close the debate; after which, the chairman immediately puts the questions to the assembly, first, on the motion to commit, if it is pending; if this is carried, of course the subject goes to the committee; if, however, it fails, the vote is next taken on amendments, and finally on the resolution as amended.

If a motion to postpone, either definitely or indefinitely, or a motion to reconsider, or an appeal is pending, the previous question is exhausted by the vote on the postponement, reconsideration or appeal, and does not cut off debate upon any other motions that may be pending. If the call for the previous question fails, that is, the debate is not cut off, the debate continues the same as if this motion had not been made. The previous question can be called for simply on an amendment, and after the amendment has been acted upon, the main question is again open to debate.

(b) *An Order limiting or closing debate.* Sometimes, instead of cutting off debate entirely by ordering the previous question, it is desirable to allow of but very limited debate. In this case, a motion is made to limit the time allowed each speaker or the number of speeches on each side, or to appoint a time at which debate shall close and the question be put. The motion may be made to limit debate on an amendment, in which case the main question would afterwards be open to debate and amendment; or it may be made simply on an amendment to an amendment.

In ordinary societies, where harmony is so important, a two-thirds vote should be required for the adoption of any of the above motions to cut off or limit debate.*

59. **To Suppress the Question.** (a) *Objection to the consideration of a question.* Sometimes a resolution is introduced that the

---

* In the House of Representatives, these motions require only a majority vote for their adoption. In the Senate, to the contrary, not even two-thirds of the members can force a measure to its passage without allowing debate, the Senate rules not recognizing the above motions.

assembly do not wish to consider at all, because it is profitless, or irrelevant to the objects of the assembly, or for other reasons. The proper course to pursue in such case, is for some one, as soon as it is introduced, to "object to the consideration of the question." This objection not requiring a second, the chairman immediately puts the question, "Will the assembly consider this question?" If decided in the negative by a two-thirds vote, the question is immediately dismissed, and cannot be again introduced during that session. This objection must be made when the question is first introduced, before it has been debated, and it can be made when another member has the floor.

(b) *Postpone indefinitely*. After the question has been debated, the proper motion to use in order to suppress the question for the session, is to postpone indefinitely. It cannot be made while any motion except the original or main question is pending, but it can be made after an amendment has been acted upon, and the main question, as amended, is before the assembly. It opens the merits of the main question to debate to as great an extent as if the main question were before the assembly. On account of these two facts, in assemblies with short sessions it is not very useful, as the same result can usually be more easily attained by the next motion.

(c) *Lie on the table*. If there is no possibility during the remainder of the session of obtaining a majority vote for taking up the question, then the quickest way of suppressing it is to move "that the question lie on the table;" which, allowing of no debate, enables the majority to instantly lay the question on the table, from which it cannot be taken without their consent.

From its high rank [§ 64] and undebatable character, this motion is very commonly used to suppress a question, but, as shown in § 57 (b), its effect is merely to lay the question aside till the assembly choose to consider it, and it only suppresses the question so long as there is a majority opposed to its consideration.

60. **To Consider a question the second time, or Reconsider**. When a question has been once adopted, rejected or suppressed, it cannot be again considered during that session [§ 70], except by

a motion to "reconsider the vote" on that question. This motion can only be made by one who voted on the prevailing side, and on the day the vote was taken which it is proposed to reconsider.* It can be made and entered on the minutes in the midst of debate, even when another member has the floor, but cannot be considered until there is no question before the assembly, when, if called up, it takes precedence of every motion except to adjourn and to fix the time to which the assembly shall adjourn.

A motion to reconsider a vote on a debatable question, opens to debate the entire merits of the original motion. If the question to be reconsidered is undebatable, then the reconsideration is undebatable. If the motion to reconsider is carried, the chairman announces that the question now recurs on the adoption of the question the vote on which has been just reconsidered: the original question is now in exactly the same condition that it was in before the first vote was taken on its adoption, and must be disposed of by a vote.

When a motion to reconsider is entered on the minutes, it need not be called up by the mover till the next meeting, on a succeeding day.† If he fails to call it up then, any one else can do so. But should there be no succeeding meeting, either adjourned or regular, within a month, then the effect of the motion to reconsider terminates with the adjournment of the meeting at which it was made, and any one can call it up at that meeting.

In general no motion (except to adjourn) that has been once acted upon, can again be considered during the same session, except by a motion to reconsider. [The motion to adjourn can be renewed if there has been progress in business or debate, and it

---

* In Congress it can be made on the same or succeeding day; and if the yeas and nays were not taken on the vote, any one can move the reconsideration. The yeas and nays are however ordered on all important votes in Congress, which is not the case in ordinary societies.

† If the assembly has not adopted these or similar rules, this paragraph would not apply, but this motion to reconsider would, like any other motion, fall to the ground if not acted upon before the close of the session at which the original vote was adopted.

cannot be reconsidered.] But this rule does not prevent the renewal of any of the motions mentioned in § 64, provided the question before the assembly has in any way changed; for in this case, while the motions are nominally the same, they are in fact different.*

61. **Order and Rules.** (a) *Orders of the Day.* Sometimes an assembly decides that certain questions shall be considered at a particular time, and when that time arrives those questions constitute what is termed the "orders of the day," and if any member "calls for the orders of the day," as it requires no second, the chairman immediately puts the question, thus: "Will the assembly now proceed to the orders of the day?" If carried, the subject under consideration is laid aside, and the questions appointed for that time are taken up in their order. When the time arrives, the chairman may state that fact, and put the above question without waiting for a motion. If the motion fails, the call for the orders of the day cannot be renewed till the subject then before the assembly is disposed of.†

---

* Thus to move to postpone a resolution is a different question from moving to postpone it after it has been amended. A motion to suspend the rules for a certain purpose cannot be renewed at the same meeting, but can be at an adjourned meeting. A call for the orders of the day that has been negatived, cannot be renewed while the question then before the assembly is still under consideration. See § 27, for many peculiarities of this motion.

† In Congress, a member entitled to the floor cannot be interrupted by a call for the orders of the day. In an ordinary assembly, the most common case where orders of the day are decided upon is where it is necessary to make a programme for the session. When the hour arrives for the consideration of any subject on the programme, these rules permit any member to call for the orders of the day (as described in § 2) even though another person has the floor. If this were not permitted, it would often be impossible to carry out the programme, though wished for by the majority. A majority could postpone the orders of the day, when called for, so as to continue the discussion of the question then before the assembly. An order as to the time when any subject shall be considered, must not be confounded with the rules of the assembly; the latter must be enforced by the chairman, without they are suspended by a two-thirds vote; the former, in strictness, can only be carried out by the order of a majority of the assembly then present and voting.

(b) *Special Order.* If a subject is of such importance that it is desired to consider it at a special time in preference to the orders of the day and established order of business, then a motion should be made to make the question a "special order" for that particular time. This motion requires a two-thirds vote for its adoption, because it is really a suspension of the rules, and it is in order whenever a motion to suspend the rules is in order. If a subject is a special order for a particular day, then on that day it supersedes all business except the reading of the minutes. A special order can be postponed by a majority vote. If two special orders are made for the same day, the one first made takes precedence.

(c) *Suspension of the Rules.* It is necessary for every assembly, if discussion is allowed, to have rules to prevent its time being wasted, and to enable it to accomplish the object for which the assembly was organized. And yet at times their best interests are subserved by suspending their rules temporarily. In order to do this, some one makes a motion "to suspend the rules that interfere with," etc., stating the object of the suspension. If this motion is carried by a two-thirds vote, then the particular thing for which the rules were suspended can be done. By "general consent," that is, if no one objects, the rules can at any time be ignored without the formality of a motion.

(d) *Questions of Order.* It is the duty of the chairman to enforce the rules and preserve order, and when any member notices a breach of order, he can call for the enforcement of the rules. In such cases, when he rises he usually says, "Mr. Chairman, I rise to a point of order." The chairman then directs the speaker to take his seat, and having heard the point of order, decides the question and permits the first speaker to resume his speech, directing him to abstain from any conduct that was decided to be out of order. When a speaker has transgressed the rules of decorum he cannot continue his speech, if any one objects, without permission is granted him by a vote of the assembly. Instead of the above method, when a member uses improper language, some one says, "I call the gentleman to order;" when the chairman decides as before whether the language is disorderly.

(e) *Appeal.* While on all questions of order, and of interpretation of the rules and of priority of business, it is the duty of the chairman to first decide the question, it is the privilege of any member to "appeal from the decision." If the appeal is seconded, the chairman states his decision, and that it has been appealed from, and then states the question, thus: "Shall the decision of the chair stand as the judgment of the assembly?" [or society, convention, etc.].

The chairman can then, without leaving the chair, state the reasons for his decision, after which it is open to debate (no member speaking but once), excepting in the following cases, when it is undebatable: (1) When it relates to transgressions of the rules of speaking, or to some indecorum, or to the priority of business; and (2) when the previous question was pending at the time the question of order was raised. After the vote is taken, the chairman states that the decision of the chair is sustained, or reversed, as the case may be.

62. **Miscellaneous**. (a) *Reading of papers* and (b) *Withdrawal of a motion*. If a speaker wishes to read a paper, or a member to withdraw his motion after it has been stated by the chair, it is necessary, if any one objects, to make a motion to grant the permission.

(c) *Questions of Privilege.* Should any disturbance occur during the meeting, or anything affecting the rights of the assembly or any of the members, any member may "rise to a question of privilege," and state the matter, which the chairman decides to be, or not to be, a matter of privilege: (from the chairman's decision of course an appeal can be taken). If the question is one of privilege, it supersedes, for the time being, the business before the assembly; its consideration can be postponed to another time, or the previous question can be ordered on it so as to stop debate, or it can be laid on the table, or referred to a committee to examine and report upon it. As soon as the question of privilege is in some way disposed of, the debate which was interrupted is resumed.

63. **To Close the Meeting**. (a) *Fix the time to which to adjourn.* If it is desired to have an adjourned meeting of the assembly, it is best some time before its close to move, "That when this assembly adjourns, it adjourns to meet at such a time," specifying the time.

This motion can be amended by altering the time, but if made when another question is before the assembly, neither the motion nor the amendment can be debated. If made when no other business is before the assembly, it stands as any other main question, and can be debated. This motion can be made even while the assembly is voting on the motion to adjourn, but not when another member has the floor.

(b) *Adjourn*. In order to prevent an assembly from being kept in session an unreasonably long time, it is necessary to have a rule limiting the time that the floor can be occupied by any one member at one time.* When it is desired to close the meeting, without the member who has the floor will yield it, the only resource is to wait till his time expires, and then a member who gets the floor should move "to adjourn." The motion being seconded, the chairman instantly put the question, as it allows of no amendment or debate; and if decided in the affirmative, he says, "The motion is carried;—this assembly stands adjourned." If the assembly is one that will have no other meeting, instead of "adjourned," he says "adjourned without day," or "sine die." If previously it had been decided when they adjourned to adjourn to a particular time, then he states that the assembly stands adjourned to that time. If the motion to adjourn is qualified by specifying the time, as, "to adjourn to to-morrow evening," it cannot be made when any other question is before the assembly; like any other main motion, it can then be amended and debated.†

64. **Order of Precedence of Motions**. The ordinary motions rank as follows, and any of them (except to amend) can be made while one of a lower order is pending, but none can supersede one of a higher order:

To Fix the Time to which to Adjourn.
To Adjourn (when unqualified).
For the Orders of the Day.

---

* Ten minutes is allowed by these rules.
† For the effect of an adjournment upon unfinished business see § 69.

To Lie on the Table.
For the Previous Question.
To Postpone to a Certain Time.
To Commit.
To Amend.
To Postpone Indefinitely.

The motion to Reconsider can be made when any other question is before the assembly, but cannot be acted upon until the business then before the assembly is disposed of; when, if called up, it takes precedence of all other motions except to adjourn and to fix the time to which to adjourn. Questions incidental to those before the assembly take precedence of them, and must be acted upon first.

A question of order, a call for the orders of the day, or an objection to the consideration of a question, can be made while another member has the floor: so, too, can a motion to reconsider, but it can only be entered on the minutes at that time, as it cannot supersede the question then before the assembly.

ART. XIII. DEBATE.

[§§ 65–66.]

65. **Rules of Speaking in Debate.** All remarks must be addressed to the chairman, and must be confined to the question before the assembly, avoiding all personalities and reflections upon any one's motives. It is usual for permanent assemblies to adopt rules limiting the number of times any member can speak to the same question, and the time allowed for each speech;* as otherwise one member, while he could speak only once to the same question, might defeat a measure by prolonging his speech and declining to yield the floor except for a motion to adjourn. In ordinary assemblies two speeches should be allowed each

---

* In Congress the House of Representatives allows from each member only one speech of one hour's length; the Senate allows two speeches without limit as to length.

member (except upon an appeal), and these rules also limit the time for each speech to ten minutes. A majority can permit a member to speak oftener or longer whenever it is desired, and the motion granting such permission cannot be debated.

However, if greater freedom is wanted, it is only necessary to consider the question informally, or if the assembly is large, go into committee of the whole. [See §§ 32, 33.] If on the other hand it is desired to limit the debate more, or close it altogether, it can be done by a two-thirds vote, as shown in § 58 (b).

66. **Undebatable Questions and those Opening the Main Question to Debate**. [A full list of these will be found in § 35, to which the reader is referred. To the undebatable motions in that list, should be added the motion to close or limit debate.]

ART. XIV. MISCELLANEOUS.

[§§ 67–73.]

67. **Forms of Stating and Putting Questions.** Whenever a motion has been made and seconded, it is the duty of the chairman, if the motion is in order, to state the question so that the assembly may know what question is before them. The seconding of a motion is required to prevent a question being introduced when only one member is in favor of it, and consequently but little attention is paid to it in mere routine motions, or when it is evident that many are in favor of the motion; in such cases the chairman assumes that the motion is seconded.

Often in routine work the chairman puts the question without waiting for even a motion, as few persons like to make such formal motions, and much time would be wasted by waiting for them: (but the chairman can only do this as long as no one objects). The following motions, however, do not have to be seconded: (a) a call for the orders of the day; (b) a call to order, or the raising of any question of order; and (c) an objection to the consideration of a question.

One of the commonest forms of stating a question is to say that, "It is moved and seconded that," and then give the motion. When an amendment has been voted on, the chairman announces the result, and then says, "The question now recurs on the resolution," or, "on the resolution as amended," as the case may be. So in all cases, as soon as a vote is taken, he should immediately state the question then before the assembly, if there be any. If the motion is debatable or can be amended, the chairman, usually after stating the question, and always before finally putting it, inquires, "Are you ready for the question?" Some of the common forms of stating and putting questions are shown in §§ 46–48. The forms of putting the following questions, are, however, peculiar:

If a motion is made to Strike out certain words, the question is put in this form: "Shall these words stand as a part of the resolution?" so that on a tie vote they are struck out.

If the Previous Question is demanded, it is put thus: "Shall the main question be now put?"

If an Appeal is made from the decision of the Chair, the question is put thus: "Shall the decision of the Chair stand as the judgment of the assembly?" [convention, society, etc.]. If the Orders of the Day are called for, the question is put thus: "Will the assembly now proceed to the Orders of the Day?"

When, upon the introduction of a question, some one objects to its consideration, the chairman immediately puts the question thus: "Will the assembly consider it?" or, "Shall the question be considered?" [or discussed].

If the vote has been ordered to be taken by yeas and nays, the question is put in a form similar to the following: "As many as are in favor of the adoption of these resolutions, will, when their names are called, answer yes [or aye]—those opposed will answer no."

68. Motions requiring a two-thirds vote.*

---

* See Two-thirds Vote, pp. 106–7, and § 39.

All motions that have the effect to make a variation from the established rules and customs, should require a two-thirds vote for their adoption. Among these established customs should be regarded the right of free debate upon the merits of any measure, before the assembly can be forced to take final action upon it. The following motions would come under this rule:

To amend or suspend the rules.
To make a special order.
To take up a question out of its proper order.
An objection to the consideration of a question.
The Previous Question, or a motion to limit or close debate.

69. **Unfinished Business.** When an assembly adjourns, the unfinished business comes up at the adjourned meeting, if one is held, as the first business after the reading of the minutes; if there is no adjourned meeting, the unfinished business comes up immediately before new business at the next regular meeting, provided the regular meetings are more frequent than yearly.* If the meetings are only once a year, the adjournment of the session puts an end to all unfinished business.

70. **Session.** Each regular meeting of a society constitutes a separate session. Any meeting which is not an adjournment of another meeting, commences a new session; the session terminates as soon as the assembly "adjourns without day."†

---

* See Rules of Order, § 11, for a fuller explanation of the effect of an adjournment upon unfinished business, and the Congressional practice.

† In ordinary practice, a meeting is closed by moving simply "to adjourn;" the society meet again at the time provided either by their rules or by a resolution of the society. If they do not meet till the time for the next regular meeting, as provided in the By-Laws, then the adjournment closed the session, and was in effect an adjournment without day. If, however, they had previously fixed the time for the next meeting, either by a direct vote, or by adopting a programme of exercises covering several meetings or even days, in either case the adjournment is in effect to a certain day, and does not close the session.

When an assembly has meetings for several days consecutively, they all constitute one session. Each session of a society is independent of the other sessions, excepting as expressly provided in their Constitution, By-Laws, or Rules of Order, and excepting that resolutions adopted by one session are in force during succeeding sessions until rescinded by a majority vote [see note to § 49].

Where a society holds more than one regular session a year, these rules limit the independence of each session as follows: (a) The Order of Business prescribed in § 72 requires that the minutes of the previous meeting, the reports of committees previously appointed, and the unfinished business of the last session, shall all take precedence of new business, and that no subject can be considered out of its proper order, except by a two-thirds vote; (b) it is allowable to postpone a question to the next session, when it comes up with unfinished business, but it is not allowable to postpone to a day beyond the next session, and thus interfere with the right of the next session to consider the question; (c) a motion to reconsider a vote can be made at one meeting and called up at the next meeting even though it be another session, provided the society holds its regular sessions as frequently as monthly.*

71. **Quorum.** [See § 43 for full information on this subject.]

72. **Order of Business.** Every society should adopt an order of business adapted to its special wants. The following is the usual order where no special rule is adopted, and when more than one regular meeting is held each year:

(1) Reading of the minutes of the last meeting.
(2) Reports of Boards of Trustees or Managers, and Standing Committees.
(3) Reports of Select Committees.
(4) Unfinished Business (including questions postponed to this meeting).
(5) New Business.

---

* See § 42, for a full discussion of this subject.

Business cannot be considered out of its order, except by a two-thirds vote; but a majority can lay on the table the different questions as they come up, and thus reach a subject they wish first to consider. If a subject has been made a Special Order for this meeting, then it is to be considered immediately after the minutes are read.

73. **Amendments of Constitutions, By-Laws and Rules of Order**, should be permitted only when adopted by a two-thirds vote, at a regular meeting of the society, after having been proposed at the previous regular meeting. If the meetings are very frequent, weekly, for instance, amendments should be adopted only at the quarterly meetings, after having been proposed at the previous quarterly meeting.

LEGAL RIGHTS OF ASSEMBLIES AND THE TRIAL OF THEIR MEMBERS.

The Right of Deliberative Assemblies to Punish their Members. A deliberative assembly has the inherent right to make and enforce its own laws and punish an offender—the extreme penalty, however, being expulsion from its own body. When expelled, if the assembly is a permanent society, it has a right, for its own protection, to give public notice that the person has ceased to be a member of that society.

But it has no right to go beyond what is necessary for self protection and publish the charges against the member. In a case where a member of a society was expelled, and an officer of the society published, by their order, a statement of the grave charges upon which he had been found guilty, the expelled member recovered damages from the officer, in a suit for libel—the court holding that the truth of the charges did not affect the case.

The Right of an Assembly to Eject any one from its place of meeting. Every deliberative assembly has the right to decide who may be present during its session, and when the assembly, either by a rule or by a vote, decides that a certain person shall not remain in the room, it is the duty of the chairman to enforce the rule or order, using whatever force is necessary to eject the party.

The chairman can detail members to remove the person, without calling upon the police. If, however, in enforcing the order, any one uses harsher treatment than is necessary to remove the person, the courts have held that he, and he alone is liable to prosecution, just the same as a policeman would be under similar circumstances. However badly the man may be abused while being removed from the room, neither the chairman nor the society are liable for damages, as, in ordering his removal, they did not exceed their legal rights.

Rights of Ecclesiastical Tribunals. Many of our deliberative assemblies are ecclesiastical bodies, and it is important to know how much respect will be paid to their decisions by the civil courts.

A church became divided and each party claimed to be the church, and therefore entitled to the church property. The case was taken into the civil courts, and finally, on appeal, to the U.S. Supreme Court, which held the case under advisement for one year, and then reversed the decision of the State Court, because it conflicted with the decision of the highest ecclesiastical court that had acted upon the case. The Supreme Court, in rendering its decision, laid down the broad principle that, when a local church is but a part of a larger and more general organization or denomination, it will accept the decision of the highest ecclesiastical tribunal to which the case has been carried within that general church organization, as final, and will not inquire into the justice or injustice of its decree as between the parties before it. The officers, the ministers, the members, or the church body which the highest judiciary of the denomination recognizes, the court will recognize. Whom that body expels or cuts off, the court will hold to be no longer members of that church.

Trial of Members of Societies. Every deliberative assembly, having the right to purify its own body, must therefore have the right to investigate the character of its members.

It can require any of them to testify in the case, under pain of expulsion if they refuse. In § 36 is shown the method of procedure when a member is charged with violating the rules of decorum in debate. If the disorderly words are of a personal nature, before the assembly proceeds to deliberate upon the case, both parties to the personality should retire. It is not necessary for the member objecting to the words to retire, unless he is personally involved in the case.

When the charge is against the member's character, it is usually referred to a committee of investigation or discipline, or to some standing committee to report upon. Some societies have standing committees, whose duty it is to report cases for discipline whenever any are known to them.

In either case the committee investigate the matter and report to the society. This report need not go into details, but should contain their recommendations as to what action the society should take, and should usually close with resolutions covering the case, so that there is no need for any one to offer any additional resolutions upon it. The ordinary resolutions, where the member is recommended to be expelled, are (1) to fix the time to which the society shall adjourn; and (2) to instruct the clerk to cite the member to appear before the society at this adjourned meeting to show cause why he should not be expelled, upon the following charges, which should then be given.

After charges are preferred against a member and the assembly has ordered that he be cited to appear for trial, he is theoretically under arrest, and is deprived of all the rights of membership until his case is disposed of.

The clerk should send the accused a written notice to appear before the society at the time appointed, and should at the same time furnish him with a copy of the charges. A failure to obey the summons is generally cause enough for summary expulsion.

At the appointed meeting, what may be called the trial, takes place. Frequently the only evidence required against the member is the report of the committee. After it has been read and any additional evidence offered that the committee may see fit to introduce, the accused should be allowed to make an explanation and introduce witnesses if he so desires. Either party should be allowed to cross-examine the other's witnesses and introduce rebutting testimony.

When the evidence is all in, the accused should retire from the room, and the society deliberate upon the question, and finally act by a vote upon the question of expulsion or other punishment proposed.

In acting upon the case, it must be borne in mind that there is a vast distinction between the evidence necessary to convict in a civil court and that required to convict in an ordinary society or ecclesiastical body. A notorious pickpocket could not even be arrested, much less convicted, by a civil court, simply on the ground of being commonly known as a pickpocket; while such evidence would convict and expel him from any ordinary society.

The moral conviction of the truth of the charge is all that is necessary in an ecclesiastical or other deliberative body, to find the accused guilty of the charges.

If the trial is liable to be long and troublesome, or of a very delicate nature, the member is frequently cited to appear before a committee, instead of the society, for trial. In this case the committee report to the society the result of their trial of the case, with resolutions covering the punishment which they recommend the society to adopt.

TABLE OF RULES RELATING TO MOTIONS.

[This Table contains the answers to more than two hundred questions on parliamentary law, and should always be consulted before referring to the body of the Manual.]

TABLE OF RULES RELATING TO MOTIONS.

Explanation of the Table. A Star shows that the rule heading the column in which it stands, applies to the motion opposite to which it is placed: a blank shows that the rule does not apply: a figure shows that the rule only partially applies, the figure referring to the note on the next page showing the limitations. Take, for example, "Lie on the table:" The Table shows that § 19 of the Pocket Manual treats of this motion; that it is "undebatable" and "cannot be amended;" and that an affirmative vote on it (as shown in note 3) "cannot be reconsidered:" —the four other columns being blank, show that this motion does not "open the main question to debate," that it does not "require a 2/3 vote," that it does "require to be seconded," and that it is not "in order when another member has the floor." The column headed "Requires a two-thirds vote," applies only where the "Pocket Manual of Rules of Order," or similar rules, have been adopted. [See "Two-thirds Vote," on page 106, under Miscellaneous Rules.] After the note to the Table is some additional information that a chairman should always have at hand, such as the Order of Precedence of Motions, the Forms of Putting Certain Questions, etc.

Section in Pocket Manual	Motion	Undebatable [§ 35]	Opens Main Question to Debate [§ 35]	Cannot be Amended [§ 23]	Cannot be Reconsidered [§ 27]	Requires a 2/3 vote [§ 39]—See Note 1.	Requires no Second [§ 3]	In order when another has the floor [§ 2]
11	Adjourn	x		x	x			
10	Adjourn, Fix the Time to which to	2						
23	Amend		x					
23	Amend an Amendment							
43	Amend the Rules					x		
14	Appeal, relating to indecorum, etc, [6]	x		x				x
14	Appeal, all other cases			x				x
14	Call to Order	x		x			x	x
37	Close Debate, motion to	x		x		x		
22	Commit		x					
31	Extend the limits of debate, motion to	x						
10	Fix the Time to which to Adjourn	2						
15	Leave to continue speaking when guilty of indecorum	x		x				
19	Lie on the Table	x		x	3			

Motion	§	1	2	3	4	5	6	7
Limit Debate, motion to	37	x					x	x
Objection to Consideration of a Question [7]	13	x		x			x	x
Orders of the Day, motion for the	13	x					x	x
Postpone to a certain time	21	4						
Postpone indefinitely	24	x	x					
Previous Question	20	x					x	
Priority of Business, questions relating to	44	x						
Reading Papers	16	x						
Reconsider a debatable question	27	x	x					5
Reconsider an undebatable question	27	x						5
Refer (same as Commit)	22		x	x				
Rise (in Committee equals Adjourn)	11	x				x		
Shall the question be discussed? [7]	11	x					x	x
Special Order, to make a	61	x				x		
Substitute (same as Amend)	23			x				
Suspend the Rules	18	x				x	x	
Take from the table	59	x		3			x	
Take up a question out of its proper order	44	x				x	x	
Withdrawal of a motion	17	x		x				

Notes to the Table.

(1) This column only applies to assemblies that have adopted these Rules. If no rules are adopted, a majority vote is sufficient for the adoption of any motion, except to "suspend the rules," which requires a unanimous vote. [See Two-thirds Vote, below.]

(2) Undebatable if made when another question is before the assembly.

(3) An affirmative vote on this motion cannot be reconsidered.

(4) Allows of but limited debate upon the propriety of the postponement. (5) Can be moved and entered on the record when another has the floor, but cannot interrupt the business then before the assembly; it must be made on the day the original vote was taken, and by one who voted with the prevailing side.

(6) An appeal is undebatable only when relating to indecorum, or to transgressions of the rules of speaking, or to the priority of business, or when made while the Previous Question is pending. When debatable, only one speech from each member is permitted.

(7) The objection can only be made when the question is first introduced, before debate.

MISCELLANEOUS RULES.

Order of Precedence of Motions.

The ordinary motions rank as follows, and any of them (except to amend) can be made while one of a lower order is pending, but none can supersede one of a higher order:

To Fix the Time to which to Adjourn.
To Adjourn (when unqualified).
For the Orders of the Day.
To Lie on the Table.
For the Previous Question.
To Postpone to a Certain Time.
To Commit.
To Amend.
To Postpone Indefinitely.

The motion to Reconsider can be made when any other question is before the assembly, but cannot be acted upon until the business then before the assembly is disposed of [see note 5 above], when, if called up, it takes precedence of all other motions except to adjourn and to fix the time to which to adjourn. Questions incidental to those before the assembly, take precedence of them and must be acted upon first.

Two-thirds Vote.

In Congress the only motions requiring a two-thirds vote, are to suspend or amend the Rules, to take up business out of its proper order, and to make a special order. In ordinary societies harmony is so essential, that a two-thirds vote should be required to force the assembly to a final vote upon a resolution without allowing free debate. The Table conforms to the Rules of Order, which are based upon this principle. If an assembly has adopted no Rules of Order, then a majority vote is sufficient for the adoption of any motion, except to "suspend the rules," which would require a unanimous vote.

Forms of Putting Certain Questions.

If a motion is made to Strike out certain words, the question is put in this form: "Shall these words stand as a part of the resolution?" so that on a tie vote they are struck out.

If the Previous Question is demanded, it is put thus: "Shall the main question now be put?"

If an Appeal is made from the decision of the Chair, the question is put thus: "Shall the decision of the Chair stand as the judgement of the assembly?" [convention, society, etc.].

If the Orders of the Day are called for, the question is put thus: "Will the assembly now proceed to the Orders of the Day?"

When, upon the introduction of a question, some one objects to its consideration, the chairman immediately puts the question thus: "Will the assembly consider it?" or "Shall the question be considered?" [or discussed].

If the vote has been ordered to be taken by yeas and nays, the question is put in a form similar to the following: "As many as are in favor of the adoption of these resolutions, will, when their names are called, answer yes [or aye]—those opposed will answer no."

Various Forms of Amendments.

An Amendment may be either (1) by "adding" or (2) by "striking out" words or paragraphs; or (3) by "striking out certain words and inserting others;" or (4) by "substituting" a different motion on the same subject; or (5) by "dividing the question" into two or more questions, so as to get a separate vote on any particular point or points.

ADDITIONS AND CORRECTIONS.

[These corrections, though mostly contained in other parts of the Manual, are also needed in the places here indicated.]

18th page, 9th line, after "§ 13" insert a star referring to this note: "See note to § 61."

36th " 2d line of last note, omit all after "reconsideration."

37th " at end of 2d line, insert "upon another day."

" " 1st line, insert a star, referring to this note: "In Congress the effect always terminates with the session, and it cannot be called up by any one but the mover, until the expiration of the time during which it is in order to move a reconsideration."

47th " 25th line, after "§ 34," insert "or limiting or closing debate."

50th " 16th line, insert a star referring to this note: "If both are personally interested. [See p. 102.]"

" last line of last note, insert "final" before "vote."

55th " add to the list in § 39 the motion "To make a special order."

INDEX.

The figures from 1 to 45 refer to sections in Part I; those greater than 45, to sections in Part II. A complete list of motions will be found in the Index, under the title Motions, list of. The arrangement of the work can be most easily seen by examining the Table of Contents [pp. 5–9]; its plan is explained in the Introduction, pp. 13–15.

SECTION.

Adjourn, motion to 11, 63b
    when in order 11, 64
    effect upon unfinished business 11, 69
    motion to "fix the time to which to adjourn"..10, 63
Amendment, motion to "amend" 23, 56a
    by "adding" or "striking out" 23, 56a
    by "striking out and inserting" 23, 56a
    by "substituting" 23, 56a
    by "dividing the question"..4, 23, 56a
    of an amendment... 23, 56a
    in committee.. 28, 53
    in committee of the whole...32
    of reports or propositions with several paragraphs.. 44, 48b
    of Rules of Order, By-Laws and Constitutions...45, 73
    motions that cannot be amended 23, 56a
Announcing the vote. See Forms.
Appeal from the decision of the chair...14, 61e
Apply, meaning of (Introduction, p. 15).
Assembly, how organized 46, 47, 48
    the word to be replaced by Society, Convention, etc., when it occurs in
      forms of questions, p. 16.
    legal rights of, pp. 100–103.
    right to punish members, p. 100.
    right to eject persons from their room, pp. 100–101.
    trial of members, pp. 102–3.
Ayes and Noes. *See* Yeas and Nays, § 38.

Ballot...38
Blanks, filling of...25
    in balloting, not to be counted..38
Boards of Trustees, Managers, etc., their reports in order when reports of standing
    committees are made...44, 72
        (See Quorum.)
Business, introduction of...1–5, 54
    order of..44, 72
    unfinished, effect of an adjournment upon....................................11, 69
        [See Priority of Business.]
By-Laws, what they should contain.. 49
    adoption of... 46a
    amendment of..45, 73

Chairman, duties of..40, 50
    election of.. 46a
    temporary...40, 47
    of a committee... 28, 53
    of committee of the whole...32
Change of Vote allowed before result is announced......................................38
Classification of Motions according to their object...................................... 55
    into Privileged, Incidental, Subsidiary, etc. 6–9
Clerk, duties of..41, 51
    additional duties of when receiving money......................................52
    election of.. 46a
Commit, motion to.. 22, 56b
Committees, appointment of... 22, 46c
    how they should be composed.. 22, 53
    object of.. 28, 53
    manner of conducting business in... 28, 53
    Reports of, their form... 29, 53
        their reception.. 30, 46c
        their adoption.. 31, 46c
        their place in the order of business...44, 72
        common errors in acting upon (note).................................. 30, 46c
    Minority Reports of, their form.. 29, 53
        to be acted upon must be moved as a substitute for the
            committee's report.. 28, 53
    of the whole..32
    as if in committee of the whole...33
Congress, rules of, the basis of this work, pp. 11–12.
Consideration of a question, objection to..15, 59a
Constitutions, what they should contain... 49

adoption of by a society 48b
    amendment of 45, 73
Convention, manner of organizing and conducting a
    meeting of 47
Credentials of delegates 47

Debate, what precedes...3, 54
    no member to speak but twice in same...34, 65
    no member to speak longer than ten minutes at one time 34, 65
    a majority can extend the number and length of speeches allowed......34, 65
    number of speeches and time allowed in Congress (note)....................34, 65
    member introducing measure has right to close 34
    list of undebatable questions...35, 66
    motions that open the main question to... 35
    principles regulating the extent of (see note) 35
    decorum in...36, 65
    closing or limiting...37, 58
Decorum in debate 36, 65
Definitions of various terms [Introduction, pp. 15–16].
Delegates, organization of a meeting of... 47
Division of the assembly..38
    of questions [see Amendment] 4, 56a

Ecclesiastical Tribunals, legal rights of, p. 101.
Election of Officers 46a, 47

Fix the time to which to Adjourn, motion to 10, 63a
Floor, how to obtain 2, 54
Forms of making motions 46, 54
    of stating and putting questions 38, 67
    of announcing the result of a vote...38, 54
    of reports of committees 29, 53
    of treasurers' reports 52
    of minutes of a meeting..41, 51
    of conducting an occasional or mass meeting 46
    of conducting a meeting of delegates 47
    of conduction a meeting to organize a society 48
    of conducting an ordinary meeting of a society.................... 48b

Incidental questions 8
Indefinite postponement..24, 59b
Informal consideration of a question 33
Introduction of Business...1–5, 54

Journal, or minutes...41, 51

Legal Rights. *See* Assembly and Ecclesiastical Tribunals.
Lie on the table, motion to...19, 57b, 59c

Main question..6
Majority. See Two-thirds and Quorum.
Meeting, distinction between it and session..42, 70
     [*See also* Introduction, pp. 15–16.]
    how to conduct. *See* Forms.
Members not to be present during a debate or vote concerning themselves...........36
    trial of, pp. 102–3.
Minority Report. See Committees.
Minutes, form and contents of..41, 51
Moderator. See Chairman.
Modification of a motion by the mover..5
Motions, list of. [For details, see each motion in the Index.]
    Adjourn 11, 63b
    Adjourn, Fix the time to which to..10, 63a
    Amend 23, 56a
    Adopt a report (same as accept or agree to) 31, 46c
    Appeal..14, 61e
    Blanks, filling 25
    Call to order..14, 61d
    Close debate 37, 58
    Commit 22, 56b
    Consideration of a question, objection to.................................15, 59a
    Divide the question...4, 23, 56a
    Extend the limits of debate...34, 65
    Fix the time to which to adjourn..10, 63a
    Incidental motions or questions...8
    Indefinitely postpone... 24, 59b
    Informal consideration of a question 33
    Leave to continue speech when guilty of indecorum 36
    Leave to withdraw a motion..17, 62b
    Lie on the table 19, 57b, 59c
    Limit Debate..37, 58b
    Main motions or questions 6
    Objection to the consideration of a question 15, 59a
    Order, questions of...14, 61d
    Orders of the day..13, 61a
    Orders, special...61b
    Postpone to a certain day..21, 57a

Postpone indefinitely...24, 59b
Previous question...20, 58a
Principal motions or questions...6
Priority of Business, questions relating to 35
Privileged motions or questions...9
Privilege, questions of.. 12, 62c
Reading papers..16, 62
Reception of a report [see Committees] 30, 46c
Recommit [same as Commit] 22, 56
Reconsider.. 27, 60
Refer [same as Commit]... 22, 56b
Renewal of a motion...26, 60
Rise [in committee, equals adjourn] 11, 32
Shall the question be considered? [or discussed] 15, 59a
Special Order, to make a 61b
Strike out [see Amendment] 23, 56a
Subsidiary motions or questions...7
Substitute (same as Amendment, which see)..............................23, 56a
Suspension of the Rules 18, 61c
Take from the table [see Lie on the table]..................................19, 57b
Take up a question out of its proper order 44, 72
Withdrawal of a motion 17, 62
Motions, tabular view of rules relating to, pp. 104–5.
    classified according to their object.. 55
    classified into Privileged, Incidental, Subsidiary, etc................................6–9
    order of precedence of [see each motion, §§ 10–27]......................... 64
    how to be made..1, 2, 46, 54
    a second required (with certain exceptions) 3, 67
    to be stated by chairman before being discussed 3, 54
    when to be in writing.. 4, 54
    how to be divided.. 4
    how to be modified by the mover 3, 5, 17
    how to be stated and put to the question.....................................38, 67
    that cannot be amended..23, 56a
    that cannot be debated..35, 66
    that open main question to debate 35
    that require two-thirds vote for their adoption 39, 68

Nominations, how treated.. 25, 46a
Numbers of paragraphs to be corrected by clerk without a vote.............................. 23

Objection to the consideration (discussion or introduction of a question.......15, 59a
Officers of an assembly. See Chairman, Clerk, Treasurer and Vice-Presidents.

Order, questions of and a call to...14, 61d
    of business...44, 72
    of the day..13, 61a
    distinction between, and rules of the assembly (note)............................. 61a
    special 61b
    of precedence of motions. See Precedence.
Organization of an occasional or mass meeting 46a
    of a convention or assembly of delegates... 47
    of a permanent society 48

Papers and documents, reading of...16, 62
    in custody of clerk 41, 51
Parliamentary Law, its origin, etc., (Introduction. p. 11.)
Plan of the Manual, (Introduction, pp. 13–15.)
    of Part I, Rules of Order, (Introduction, pp. 14–15.)
    of Part II, Organization and Conduct of Business,
        (Introduction, p. 15.)
Postpone to a certain time...21, 57a
    indefinitely..24, 59b
Preamble, considered after the rest of a paper.. 44
Precedence of motions [see each motion, §§ 10–27]................................. 64
    meaning of, (Introduction, p. 15.)
Presiding Officer. See Chairman.
Previous Question 20, 58a
Principal (or main) question..6
Priority of Business, questions relating to are undebatable..................... 35
Privilege, questions of 12, 62c
Privileged questions 9
Putting the question, form of...38, 67

Questions. See Forms, Motions, Privilege and Order.
Quorum, when there is no rule, consists of a majority................................43
    committees and boards cannot decide upon 43

Reading of Papers..16, 62
Reception of a report. See Committees.
Re-commit (same as Commit) 22, 56b
Reconsider...27, 60
Record, or minutes 41, 51
Recording officer. See Clerk.
Refer [same as Commit]... 22, 56b
Renewal of a motion..26, 60
Reports of committees. See Committees.
Rights of assemblies. See Assembly.
    of ecclesiastical tribunals, p. 101.

Rise, motion to, in committee, equals adjourn.. 11, 32
Rules of debate. See Debate.
       of Order, amendment of 45, 73
       of Order, what they should contain 49
       standing, what they should contain... 49
       suspension of...18, 61c
       relating to motions, tabular view of pp. 104–5.

Seconding, motions that do not require..3, 67
Secretary. *See* Clerk.
Session [*See also* Meeting] 42, 70
Shall the question be considered (or discussed) 15, 59a
Speaking, rules of, See Debate.
Special Order 61b
Standing Rules.. 49
Stating a question, form of..38, 67
Strike out (see Amendment).. 23, 56a
Subsidiary motions or questions 7
Substitute (see Amendment) 23, 56a
Sum, largest, first put 25
Suspension of the rules 18, 61c

Table of Rules relating to motions, pp. 104–5.
Take from the table, motion to.. 19, 57b
Time, longest, first put 25
Treasurer, duties of..52
Trial of Members, pp. 102–3.
Two-thirds vote, motions requiring 39, 68

Undebatable Questions 35, 66
Unfinished business, effect of adjournment upon.................................11, 69
       its place in the order of business... 44, 72

Vice-Presidents   46d
Vote, form of announcing [see also Forms]..38, 54
       motions requiring more than a majority 39, 68
       change of, permitted before result is announced 38
Voting, various methods of...38

Withdrawal of a motion 17, 62

Yeas and Nays, voting by...38
Yields, meaning of, (Introduction, p. 15.)

ACKNOWLEDGMENTS

This book turned out to be a perfect pandemic project, whisking me away to a distant time and place and giving me lots of new and fascinating history to think about and learn. Peter Dougherty at Princeton University Press invited me to take on this assignment. I'm glad he did. The Library of Congress bolstered my faith in government (again!) by lending me a microfilmed copy of the Henry M. Robert Papers. Anne Jarvis and Dan Linke at Princeton University Library helped answer a last-minute research question. Three generous peer reviewers offered incisive suggestions that improved the analysis. Derek Hoff provided comments on an early draft, and Brian Balogh, as always, on several later ones. Catherine Gavin Loss's deft touch and keen eye makes everything better. Princeton's crack production team, in particular Terri O'Prey and Anne Sanow, spiffed up the book as only they can. Of course, any remaining errors of fact or interpretation are mine alone. My mom, Suzanne Perry Loss, gets the last word. When I was growing up, she had mercifully few rules but was a real stickler for order. This book is for her—with love.

—CPL
Nashville, Tennessee